HAPPINESS
STRESS DOWN

Also by Aleks George Srbinoski

Destiny Defining Decisions: Best-Selling Entrepreneurs Reveal their
Greatest Success Secrets

60 Minute Success Secrets Series Books

Motivation Now

Instant Inner Calm

10 Life Success Secrets Revealed

Precision Language

The 7 Mental Viruses Crushing Your Potential

To be released in 2015

The Mental Health and Happiness Book Series

Books can be found on Amazon or mass copies directly sought from the
author.

Happiness Up Stress Down

Increase Happiness and Decrease Stress
in just 2 Minutes a Day over 2 Weeks
and Help your Community

Aleks George Srbinoski

FULFILLING HAPPINESS PUBLISHING

Disclaimer

The author, contributors and publisher shall have neither liability nor responsibility to any person or entity with respect to any of the information, strategies or exercises contained in this document. The user assumes all risk for any injury, loss or damage caused or alleged to be caused, directly or indirectly by using any information, strategies or exercises described in the "Happiness Up Stress Down" book and related materials. All information is generalist in nature. Should any reader make use of information contained herein, this is their decision, and the contributors (and their companies), authors and publishers do not assume any responsibilities whatsoever under any circumstances or conditions.

Copyright

1st ed.
ISBN 978-0-9925826-1-6

For my father who always told me to "keep going." I will!

Acknowledgements

Thank you to the Elonera Montessori School staff and volunteers who helped run the challenge. You did an amazing job!

To my Dutchess, you are my true north and always the greatest source of assistance.

To my family, thanks to you, "little Aleks" might actually be growing up!

As for all my friends and clients of the past, present and future, may the inspiration I draw from our encounters return to you tenfold.

Contents

Introduction

What if you could improve your happiness by more than 20% and reduce stress by more than 20% in just two weeks and in less than two minutes a day?

Furthermore, what if by spending a whole 28 minutes or so total over two weeks on these specialist psychological exercises also improved your relationships and ability to positively impact friends, family, colleagues and even the greater community?

If it sounds too good to be true, then it probably is! Right? Well, maybe not this time. *I believe you may be able to become happier and less stressed by even greater percentages mentioned.* I'll explain why after a quick personal introduction.

My name is Aleks George Srbinoski (Aleks George for short) and I am an Australian Clinical Psychologist and Happiness Expert. I have previously created my own television show on happiness and have contributed as a mental illness and happiness expert in the past to major newspapers, magazines and radio in both Australia and USA.

In fact, the 102 extra happiness tips, in part two of this book, are from a selection of segments I created and were broadcast for the leading news radio program in Chicago. Pretty cool considering that at the time of writing I still had never been to the USA! I do plan to change that soon.

In part three of this book, I offer a selection of my best short happiness articles. I originally planned to offer 10, and then I added an extra companion article to the final one. I then decided to give away two more.

However, the main focus of the book is what you discover in part one, where I reveal the Happiness Up, Stress Down Challenge. I am not going to explain the neuroscience behind the challenges here, as I talk about most of the happiness principles in greater detail in part three of the book. Instead, I will be succinct in outlining the psychology behind how the challenge works.

Although the challenge can be successfully run at any time of the year, it was originally designed to be a positive twist on New Year's Resolutions. Since the end goal of a resolution is an increase in happiness, I thought why not specifically teach people how to actually be happier from the start! However, I decided to add a special bonus chapter on goal setting at the end from one of my upcoming books for those who want some extra guidance with their traditional goals and resolutions as well.

The purpose of the challenge is to create a *three stage virtuous circle of positive influence*. The first stage is simple enough. You do a 60-120 second happiness booster exercise which should lead you to feeling happier and less stressed. Because emotions are contagious, the people you interact with afterwards should feel happier too. The third stage is optional, but highly recommended.

Countless studies have shown that giving tends to increase happiness. Therefore, I encourage you to obtain sponsorship to do the challenge (to get people to actually sponsor you to become happier) and/or give away some of your money or time as well to your favorite community cause or charity. Now your efforts to become happier and less stressed will move beyond your immediate social circles and help people you probably don't even know!

Previous Results

The challenge has been successfully tested three times previously. The first test involved a close friend and I completing each 60-90 second challenge three times a day for two weeks. We both found it highly beneficial but of course people could argue that we are biased.

The second time a technology company tested the challenge. I received fantastic feedback from different participants such as…

"All in all mate I think taking 90 seconds out of your day to focus on being happy is a winner with me..."

"I like this one; I remembered my wedding day, to be exact when my wife walked through the door... wonderful thoughts."

"I am learning some good techniques here for not only being happy but in remembering what is really important in my life."

"The slow, steady breathing calmed me almost to the point of being in a trance. It really slowed me down, which was a good thing. It's something that I continue to do anytime I feel things are getting on top of me."

However, no statistical analysis was obtained.

In order to solve this problem, I went to the Elonera Montessori School in my home town of Wollongong and had the challenge independently tested on a group of students and some of the teachers. I created the scripts and it was run without my involvement.

Ideally, the challenge should run for three weeks and each challenge is done three times a day, every day. This still would only equate to five or so minutes a day spent on the exercises. Of course, this would not be practical in a school group setting so the challenge was really put to the test.

It became one 2-minute exercise done once a day, over the course of three school weeks. One school day was missed due to an excursion. Therefore, 14 challenges were completed over a 19 day period. To participate, students had to pay a fee with all proceeds going to a local charity.

This was not ideal, as it would be better if the challenge was run every day over a 2-week period minimum. For confidentiality reasons, students also had the exercises read to them (and sometimes information was forgotten). Since you will have it in front of you, you should have no problems understanding what to do. There were not enough teachers participating for meaningful results to be tabulated.

Students ranged from 11 to 16 years of age, with most being between 13 and 15. **The average overall improvement in happiness scores by the end of the challenge was 24% and the average overall reduction in stress scores was 23%.** I assume the improvement percentages would have been higher if I had received more forms, especially considering that some of the top improvement percentage scores obtained after each challenge were much higher than this.

I will reveal best Elonera Montessori student improvement percentage scores and comments after each challenge as we proceed.

Final Note before We Begin

My aim with this challenge is to increase social happiness. This book is written for the individual. However, I have all the necessary scripts required to run the challenge in a group setting. If after reading this book you feel that your organization or school would benefit from doing the challenge as a group, feel free to contact me.

It does not matter where you are in the world, as long as you meet my criteria, I will happily give you the scripts. My criterion has nothing to do with how much money your school or organization has, but rather if you can prove to me that you are willing to run the challenge properly. If so, I'll be happy to share all the materials with you.

Lastly, if you want an example of one exercise in action before you begin to get the right feeling of how you should approach the challenge, you can view my short video that explains it all with the following link –

http://ow.ly/GgK4h

You can contact me anytime. To contact me, you can use the contact tab at HappinessUpStressDown.com. You can also go there to explore the latest information about the challenge and bonus materials.

Or email me at my main address: aleks@fulfillinghappiness.com.

Let's begin!

Part 1

Happiness Up, Stress Down Challenge

How You Work

Welcome to the *Happiness Up, Stress Down Challenge*. Before you begin the challenge, it is important to explain to you how the exercises work and what you need to do to prepare yourself to get the maximum benefit from each exercise.

Happiness is an emotion. To be more precise, happiness is the generalized term for any positive emotion or emotions you may be feeling at a particular time. These could include emotions like joy, bliss, ecstasy, love, confidence and so on.

Increasing your positive emotion levels on a consistent basis such as 1-3 times a day and for a short period of time such as 7-21 days, will assist you to become happier overall. Increasing positive emotion should also lead to the decreasing of negative emotion such as stress.

To create a positive emotion – you have to change the way you are thinking, using your body and acting.

Thinking refers not just to the words you use in your mind but can also be images or memories.
Body refers to how you position your body, head, face and breathing.
Acting refers to the kind of specific behaviors you do consistently.

By thinking, acting and using your body in a certain way, you will feel happier. Done consistently over time, you will become happier.

Time & Focus: All challenges also have a particular time focus. Some will get you to utilize a past time to feel happier, some will ask you to focus on the present and others will ask you to focus on the future. Some may combine your time focus.

Simple Summary: To feel happier, you must manipulate your thinking, body and actions and focus on a particular event/s from the past, present or future.

Keeping that in mind – this is the preparation procedure I want you to go through before each challenge.

After reading each 60-90 second exercise, you will prepare yourself fully before beginning. You can always go for longer with each exercise if you like, but always rate yourself based on how you felt at the end of the scheduled time.

You will do this by sitting or standing straight and begin breathing deeply. Close your eyes and focus on letting go of any particular worries or concerns or doubts you have. Perhaps imagine your thoughts evaporating. Breathing deep, smile and promise yourself to commit fully to the challenge. Breathe, be calm, get ready and then begin!

This whole process with practice should only take a few seconds, though it may take a little longer in the beginning as you get used to it.

MEASURE OF OVERALL HAPPINESS –
Before Challenge - By Aleks George Srbinoski
May be re-printed for personal use only.

Name and/or Identification Number

_____

Date _____ Age _____ Gender _____

1. On average, how happy as a person am I?

(1 = very unhappy and 10 = extremely happy)

Score: _____

2. On average, how stressed do I feel each day?

(1 = very little and 10 = extremely stressed)

Score: _____

Daily Happiness and Stress Measure before & after each Challenge
by Aleks George Srbinoski

Name and/or Identification Number

_____

Date _____ Age _____ Gender _____

Name: Imagery Immersion

Before Challenge

On a scale of 1-10, how happy am I feeling?

(1 = very unhappy and 10 = extremely happy)

Score: _____

On a scale of 1-10, how stressed am I feeling?

(1 = very little and 10 = extremely stressed)

Score: _____

Challenge 1: Imagery Immersion

Past-focused exercise

Time: 90 seconds

Requirements: Nothing

Exercise Preparation: Sit or stand straight and begin breathing deeply. Close your eyes and focus on letting go of any particular worries, concerns or doubts you have. Perhaps imagine your thoughts evaporating. With each breath, feel centered, smile and promise yourself to commit fully to the challenge. Once committed, open your eyes, keep your smile, and continue to feel centered and breathing deeply.

Instructions: Think of one or two of your absolute favorite experiences. For younger people it may be playing and winning a game, having a party, a special moment with family or friends, or something that was really fun like being on a slide or a ride. For adults it may be a wedding day, graduation, first kiss, making love, winning at something, a fantastic conversation, a thrilling experience – any experience at all that you really enjoyed.

Rationale: The point of this exercise is that you CAN USE YOUR PAST TO EXPERIENCE HAPPINESS NOW!

Process: Once you have one or two, choose the most exciting experience, close your eyes and prepare to go through the experience again as if it was happening now. Smile and focus on your senses as you go through the experience, noticing the sights, sounds, smells, touches and tastes. Sink into the experience with each breath and immerse yourself fully as if it is happening now.

Make sure you follow your exercise preparation routine and understand the instructions. If not, read everything again and BEGIN!

30 seconds after exercise: Now close your eyes and imagine having what you feel now stay with you when you talk to friends, students, teachers, parents and anyone else you spend time with today. If completing charity component, know that you becoming happier is also raising money to help others too. Imagine how they must feel to know you're helping them as well.

After Challenge 1

On a scale of 1-10, how happy am I feeling?

(1 = very unhappy and 10 = extremely happy)

Score: _____

On a scale of 1-10, how stressed am I feeling?

(1 = very little and 10 = extremely stressed)

Score: _____

Optional Question 1: What did you like and/or dislike about this challenge?

_____
_____
_____
_____

Optional Question 2: Did you learn anything you could use in the future? If so, what?

_____
_____
_____
_____

Highest % Happiness Boost Recorded: 67% by 12-year-old female

Largest % Stress Decrease Recorded: 67% by 13-year-old female

Best Comment: Stop and chill out!

Daily Happiness and Stress Measure before & after each Challenge

Name and/or Identification Number

_____

Date _____ Age _____ Gender _____

Name: Mindful Munch

Before Challenge

On a scale of 1-10, how happy am I feeling?

(1 = very unhappy and 10 = extremely happy)

Score: _____

On a scale of 1-10, how stressed am I feeling?

(1 = very little and 10 = extremely stressed)

Score: _____

Challenge 2: Mindful Munch

Present-focused exercise

Time: 90 seconds

Requirements: A small piece of food that can easily fit in your mouth

Exercise Preparation: Sit or stand straight and begin breathing deeply. Close your eyes and focus on letting go of any particular worries, concerns or doubts you have. Perhaps imagine your thoughts evaporating. With each breath, feel centered, smile and promise yourself to commit fully to the challenge. Once committed, open your eyes, keep your smile, and continue to feel centered and breathing deeply.

Instructions: Grab a piece of food—anything that can easily fit into your mouth such as one to two pieces of chocolate, a small cut of fruit or vegetable, a piece of candy, a raisin, a nut or anything that will fit easily into your mouth.

Rationale: The point of this exercise is that YOU CAN ENJOY THE PLEASURE OF EATING MUCH MORE WHEN DONE SLOWLY AND THOUGHTFULLY!

Process: Bring the piece of food to your nose and smell it slowly letting the aroma flow into you. Then close your eyes and gently rub it against your lips for a second or two before putting it in your mouth. Focus totally on the way it feels in your mouth. Notice the flavor seeping out of the food and pooling in the back of your throat and notice the taste each time you swallow. After about 30 seconds, bite into the piece of food once very slowly and notice the burst of flavor. After another 5 seconds, bite it again slowly and then again after another 5 seconds. Then slowly chew the piece of food noticing the flavor burst out of it each time before finally swallowing it.

Make sure you follow your exercise preparation routine and understand the instructions. If not, read everything again and BEGIN!

30 seconds after exercise: Now close your eyes and imagine having what you feel now stay with you when you talk to friends, students, teachers, parents and anyone else you spend time with today. If completing charity component, know that you becoming happier is also raising money to help others too. Imagine how they must feel to know you're helping them as well.

After Challenge 2

On a scale of 1-10, how happy am I feeling?

(1 = very unhappy and 10 = extremely happy)

Score: _____

On a scale of 1-10, how stressed am I feeling?

(1 = very little and 10 = extremely stressed)

Score: _____

Optional Question 1: What did you like and/or dislike about this challenge?

_____
_____
_____
_____

Optional Question 2: Did you learn anything you could use in the future? If so, what?

_____
_____
_____
_____

Highest % Happiness Boost Recorded: 60% by 12-year-old female

Largest % Stress Decrease Recorded: 67% by 14-year-old male

Best Comment: Be more and more mindful.

Daily Happiness and Stress Measure before & after each Challenge

Name and/or Identification Number

_____

Date _____ Age _____ Gender _____

Name: Growing Gratitude

Before Challenge

On a scale of 1-10, how happy am I feeling?

(1 = very unhappy and 10 = extremely happy)

Score: _____

On a scale of 1-10, how stressed am I feeling?

(1 = very little and 10 = extremely stressed)

Score: _____

Challenge 3: Growing Gratitude

Past or Present-focused exercise

Time: 90 seconds

Requirements: Nothing or a piece of paper and pen

Exercise Preparation: Sit or stand straight and begin breathing deeply. Close your eyes and focus on letting go of any particular worries, concerns or doubts you have. Perhaps imagine your thoughts evaporating. With each breath, feel centered, smile and promise yourself to commit fully to the challenge. Once committed, open your eyes, keep your smile, and continue to feel centered and breathing deeply.

Instructions: You are going to give thanks for either the things you have, the experiences you have had or the people in your life. You can be grateful for anything: a sunrise, a type of food, a loved one, a fun time, having a particular object, your heart beat, your breath, your brain, it does not matter.

Rationale: The point of this exercise is that YOU CAN BE GRATEFUL FOR ANYTHING!

Process: Once you begin say out loud and write down everything that you are grateful for as fast as you can. Remember, it can be anything. If it pops up in your head and it is positive, then be grateful for it, say it out loud and write it down. You must do this for at least a minute. After 60-90 seconds, review your list and smile.

Make sure you follow your exercise preparation routine and understand the instructions. If not, read everything again and BEGIN!

30 seconds after exercise: Now close your eyes and imagine having what you feel now stay with you when you talk to friends, students, teachers, parents and anyone else you spend time with today. If completing charity component, know that you becoming happier is also raising money to help others too. Imagine how they must feel to know you're helping them as well.

After Challenge 3

On a scale of 1-10, how happy am I feeling?

(1 = very unhappy and 10 = extremely happy)

Score: _____

On a scale of 1-10, how stressed am I feeling?

(1 = very little and 10 = extremely stressed)

Score: _____

Optional Question 1: What did you like and/or dislike about this challenge?

_____
_____
_____
_____

Optional Question 2: Did you learn anything you could use in the future? If so, what?

_____
_____
_____
_____

Highest % Happiness Boost Recorded: 67% by 14-year-old male

Largest % Stress Decrease Recorded: 100% by 15-year-old male

Best Comment: This was fun, I enjoyed this!

Daily Happiness and Stress Measure before & after each Challenge

Name and/or Identification Number

_____

Date _____ Age _____ Gender _____

Name: Favorable Future

Before Challenge

On a scale of 1-10, how happy am I feeling?

(1 = very unhappy and 10 = extremely happy)

Score: _____

On a scale of 1-10, how stressed am I feeling?

(1 = very little and 10 = extremely stressed)

Score: _____

Challenge 4: Favorable Future

Future-focused exercise

Time: 90 seconds

Requirements: Nothing

Exercise Preparation: Sit or stand straight and begin breathing deeply. Close your eyes and focus on letting go of any particular worries, concerns or doubts you have. Perhaps imagine your thoughts evaporating. With each breath, feel centered, smile and promise yourself to commit fully to the challenge. Once committed, open your eyes, keep your smile, and continue to feel centered and breathing deeply.

Instructions: Think of 1 or 2 things you would like to happen in the future. It might be doing well on a test or in a game, maybe a holiday, or meeting and having fun with someone special. It can be anything at all that you want to happen.

Rationale: The point of this exercise is that YOU DON'T HAVE TO WAIT TO ENJOY A POSSIBLE EVENT NOW. By already having practiced enjoying it, you are more likely TO MAKE IT HAPPEN THAT WAY!

Process: You will choose one situation you would like to have happen in the future and imagine it going perfectly. You will close your eyes go through the experience as if it is happening right now. Smile and focus on your senses as you go through the experience, noticing the sights, sounds, smells, touches and tastes. Imagine the experience getting stronger every time you breathe and that you are really enjoying it as if it is happening right now.

Make sure you follow your exercise preparation routine and understand the instructions. If not, read everything again and BEGIN!

30 seconds after exercise: Now close your eyes and imagine having what you feel now stay with you when you talk to friends, students, teachers, parents and anyone else you spend time with today. If completing charity component, know that you becoming happier is also raising money to help others too. Imagine how they must feel to know you're helping them as well.

After Challenge 4

On a scale of 1-10, how happy am I feeling?

(1 = very unhappy and 10 = extremely happy)

Score: _____

On a scale of 1-10, how stressed am I feeling?

(1 = very little and 10 = extremely stressed)

Score: _____

Optional Question 1: What did you like and/or dislike about this challenge?

_____

_____

_____

_____

Optional Question 2: Did you learn anything you could use in the future? If so, what?

_____

_____

_____

_____

Highest % Happiness Boost Recorded: 43% by 13-year-old female

Largest % Stress Decrease Recorded: 33% by 13-year-old female

Best Comment (Teacher): I loved the chance to fully focus on something. Normally I don't give enough time to just thinking/being. Thinking about these future events can be so emotional - in a positive way.

Daily Happiness and Stress Measure before & after each Challenge

Name and/or Identification Number

_____

Date _____ Age _____ Gender _____

Name: Precise Praise

Before Challenge

On a scale of 1-10, how happy am I feeling?

(1 = very unhappy and 10 = extremely happy)

Score: _____

On a scale of 1-10, how stressed am I feeling?

(1 = very little and 10 = extremely stressed)

Score: _____

Challenge 5: Precise Praise

Future and by extension present-focused exercise

Time: 60-90 seconds

Name: Precise Praise

Requirements: Piece of paper and by extension a social setting with another person involved.

Exercise Preparation: Sit or stand straight and begin breathing deeply. Close your eyes and focus on letting go of any particular worries, concerns or doubts you have. Perhaps imagine your thoughts evaporating. With each breath, feel centered, smile and promise yourself to commit fully to the challenge. Once committed, open your eyes, keep your smile, and continue to feel centered and breathing deeply.

Instructions: Think of three people who are important to you and do good things for you. You are going to write down all the good things they do for you: how they have helped you or made you feel good and the fun experiences you have shared for example. Imagine saying those nice things to that person as you write it down. That is the challenge. However, next time you see that person, you are going to thank them for those experiences. For example, you might thank your mother for a recent dinner or your friend for helping you with a problem or having a great time doing an activity together.

The secret behind praise is that the comment be spoken in a genuine way and specifically address a particular thing they have done.

e.g. Unspecific praise – You are a nice person.
  You look good.
  Good (or Great) report.

e.g Specific praise – I notice you always say please and thank you; that
    is a great quality.
  You have a great sense of fashion; blue is definitely your color.
  It must have taken you ages to compile this data and make it so
    simple to read, fantastic job; I fully appreciate your effort.

Rationale: The point of this exercise is that people enjoy being appreciated. It creates greater harmony in relationships, and it feels good. They will often return the favor and praise you. This can lead to an amplification of good feelings between the people involved.

Process: Spend 90 seconds now thinking about the person with whom you want to have this enjoyable conversation and write down one piece of Genuine Precise Praise that you could say to him or her. It could be about anything they have done in the past or more recently that you appreciated. Enjoy creating it! That is the exercise as far as the challenge goes. Then do it again with someone else and a third time with another person.

Make sure you follow your exercise preparation routine and understand the instructions. If not, read everything again and BEGIN!

30 seconds after exercise: Now close your eyes and imagine having what you feel now stay with you when you talk to friends, students, teachers, parents and anyone else you spend time with today. If completing charity component, know that you becoming happier is also raising money to help others too. Imagine how they must feel to know you're helping them as well.

Extension: When the opportunity arises, I want you to have a short 60-90 second or more conversation with that person and offer the praise you wrote down. No matter what make sure you say it. If you need, just use this line at any point, "You know I was thinking about (the event) and I just wanted to say…"

After Challenge 5

On a scale of 1-10, how happy am I feeling?

(1 = very unhappy and 10 = extremely happy)

Score: _____

On a scale of 1-10, how stressed am I feeling?

(1 = very little and 10 = extremely stressed)
Score: _____

Optional Question 1: What did you like and/or dislike about this challenge?

_____
_____
_____
_____

Optional Question 2: Did you learn anything you could use in the future? If so, what?

_____
_____
_____
_____

Highest % Happiness Boost Recorded: 33% by 13-year-old female

Largest % Stress Decrease Recorded: 33% by 13-year-old female

Best Comment: …Remembering the teacher talking about my flash mob.

Daily Happiness and Stress Measure before & after each Challenge

Name and/or Identification Number

Date _____ Age _____ Gender _____

Name: Pleasurable Performing

Before Challenge

On a scale of 1-10, how happy am I feeling?

(1 = very unhappy and 10 = extremely happy)

Score: _____

On a scale of 1-10, how stressed am I feeling?

(1 = very little and 10 = extremely stressed)

Score: _____

Challenge 6: Pleasurable Performing

Present-focused exercise

Time: 90 seconds

Requirements: Nothing

Exercise Preparation: Sit or stand straight and begin breathing deeply. Close your eyes and focus on letting go of any particular worries, concerns or doubts you have. Perhaps imagine your thoughts evaporating. With each breath, feel centered, smile and promise yourself to commit fully to the challenge. Once committed, open your eyes, keep your smile, and continue to feel centered and breathing deeply.

Instructions: Think of a time when you felt really happy. Notice how you were moving, speaking and what you were doing. Notice how it felt and the kind of thoughts you were having at the time. Once you feel that person in you, you are going to act out and be that person for 90 seconds.

Rationale: The point of this exercise is that you CAN ACT HAPPY IN ORDER TO FEEL HAPPIER!

Process: If you are in a social setting, you are going to act completely happy for at least 90 seconds around other people. If you are on your own, you are going to pretend you are around other people and act completely happy for 90 seconds.

Make sure you follow your exercise preparation routine and understand the instructions. If not, read everything again and BEGIN!

30 seconds after exercise: Now close your eyes and imagine having what you feel now stay with you when you talk to friends, students, teachers, parents and anyone else you spend time with today. If completing charity component, know that you becoming happier is also raising money to help others too. Imagine how they must feel to know you're helping them as well.

Extension: Pick three people you will soon spend time with and just before you meet them next, imagine that time you were happy and feel it again. Then have a conversation with that person.

After Challenge 6

On a scale of 1-10, how happy am I feeling?

(1 = very unhappy and 10 = extremely happy)

Score: _____

On a scale of 1-10, how stressed am I feeling?

(1 = very little and 10 = extremely stressed)

Score: _____

Optional Question 1: What did you like and/or dislike about this challenge?

_____

_____

_____

_____

Optional Question 2: Did you learn anything you could use in the future? If so, what?

_____

_____

_____

_____

Highest % Happiness Boost Recorded: 42% by 15-year-old male

Largest % Stress Decrease Recorded: 60% by 13-year-old female

Best Comment: I liked remembering happy times.

Daily Happiness and Stress Measure before & after each Challenge

Name and/or Identification Number

_____

Date _____ Age _____ Gender _____

Name: Love List

Before Challenge

On a scale of 1-10, how happy am I feeling?

(1 = very unhappy and 10 = extremely happy)

Score: _____

On a scale of 1-10, how stressed am I feeling?

(1 = very little and 10 = extremely stressed)

Score: _____

Challenge 7: Love List

Present and past-focused exercise

Time: 60-90 seconds

Requirements: Piece of paper and pen

Exercise Preparation: Sit or stand straight and begin breathing deeply. Close your eyes and focus on letting go of any particular worries, concerns or doubts you have. Perhaps imagine your thoughts evaporating. With each breath, feel centered, smile and promise yourself to commit fully to the challenge. Once committed, open your eyes, keep your smile, and continue to feel centered and breathing deeply.

Instructions: You are going to think of everyone you love and anyone who has done something towards you that could be considered loving and write their name down.

Rationale: The point of this exercise is that you will see that there are a lot of great people and LOVING ACTS that have occurred in your life.

Process: Each time you write down a name, breathe deep, smile and quickly think of something loving about them or something loving they once did. Do not get too caught up with the word love. It scares some people. Any act of kindness is an act of love. Once you exhaust the classic examples of loved ones, think deeper. It might be a particular school teacher, sports coach or neighbor that has shown acts of loving kindness towards you that you can now feel and acknowledge.

Make sure you follow your exercise preparation routine and understand the instructions. If not, read everything again and BEGIN!

30 seconds after exercise: Now close your eyes and imagine having what you feel now stay with you when you talk to friends, students, teachers, parents and anyone else you spend time with today. If completing charity component, know that you becoming happier is also raising money to help others too. Imagine how they must feel to know you're helping them as well.

After Challenge 7

On a scale of 1-10, how happy am I feeling?

(1 = very unhappy and 10 = extremely happy)
Score: _____

On a scale of 1-10, how stressed am I feeling?

(1 = very little and 10 = extremely stressed)

Score: _____

Optional Question 1: What did you like and/or dislike about this challenge?

_____
_____
_____
_____

Optional Question 2: Did you learn anything you could use in the future? If so, what?

_____
_____
_____
_____

Highest % Happiness Boost Recorded: 40% by 12-year-old female

Largest % Stress Decrease Recorded: 100% by 15-year-old male

Best Comment: I liked everything in the love list actually. Thank you.

Daily Happiness and Stress Measure before & after each Challenge

Name and/or Identification Number

Date _____ Age _____ Gender _____

Name: Dynamic Dancing

Before Challenge

On a scale of 1-10, how happy am I feeling?

(1 = very unhappy and 10 = extremely happy)

Score: _____

On a scale of 1-10, how stressed am I feeling?

(1 = very little and 10 = extremely stressed)

Score: _____

Challenge 8: Dynamic Dancing

Present-focused exercise

Time: 90 seconds

Requirements: Nothing – music if available

Exercise Preparation: Sit or stand straight and begin breathing deeply. Close your eyes and focus on letting go of any particular worries, concerns or doubts you have. Perhaps imagine your thoughts evaporating. With each breath, feel centered, smile and promise yourself to commit fully to the challenge. Once committed, open your eyes, keep your smile, and continue to feel centered and breathing deeply.

Instructions: Today you are going to feel the full joy of dancing with full abandon. It is not good enough to just dance, you must do it with the spirit of complete freedom.

Rationale: The point of this exercise is that happy feelings are generated from being active. The more active you are, the HAPPIER YOU WILL FEEL!

Process: Choose one of your favorite positive, upbeat songs. If you have it available play it, if not run it through your mind, or better yet – sing it! Then, for a full 90 seconds, or more if you like, DANCE! The more reckless, wild and untamed– the better. If possible find a partner, EMOTIONS ARE CONTAGIOUS.

Make sure you follow your exercise preparation routine and understand the instructions. If not, read everything again and BEGIN!

30 seconds after exercise: Now close your eyes and imagine having what you feel now stay with you when you talk to friends, students, teachers, parents and anyone else you spend time with today. If completing charity component, know that you becoming happier is also raising money to help others too. Imagine how they must feel to know you're helping them as well.

After Challenge 8

On a scale of 1-10, how happy am I feeling?

(1 = very unhappy and 10 = extremely happy)

Score: _____

On a scale of 1-10, how stressed am I feeling?

(1 = very little and 10 = extremely stressed)

Score: _____

Optional Question 1: What did you like and/or dislike about this challenge?

_____

_____

_____

_____

Optional Question 2: Did you learn anything you could use in the future? If so, what?

_____

_____

_____

_____

Highest % Happiness Boost Recorded: 100% by 11-year-old male

Largest % Stress Decrease Recorded: 100% by 15-year-old male

Best Comment: It was fun/funny. I enjoyed it. Doesn't matter, making yourself look like a fool to make others happy.

Daily Happiness and Stress Measure before & after each Challenge

Name and/or Identification Number

_____

Date _____ Age _____ Gender _____

Name: Fantastic Future

Before Challenge

On a scale of 1-10, how happy am I feeling?

(1 = very unhappy and 10 = extremely happy)

Score: _____

On a scale of 1-10, how stressed am I feeling?

(1 = very little and 10 = extremely stressed)

Score: _____

Challenge 9: Fantastic Future

Future-focused exercise

Time: 90 seconds

Requirements: Nothing

Exercise Preparation: Sit or stand straight and begin breathing deeply. Close your eyes and focus on letting go of any particular worries, concerns or doubts you have. Perhaps imagine your thoughts evaporating. With each breath, feel centered, smile and promise yourself to commit fully to the challenge. Once committed, open your eyes, keep your smile, and continue to feel centered and breathing deeply.

Instructions: Think about all your dreams, desires and wishes. Imagine being, doing and having whatever it is that you want. Be bold and dream big if you like. Once you have accessed that general feeling of abundance visualize, experience and feel those things coming true.

Rationale: The point of this exercise is that you can enjoy visualizing and experiencing your future desires and successes now and FEEL HAPPY ABOUT THEM NOW!

Process: Close your eyes and start by imagining what you could achieve, enjoy, and experience three months from now and feel it fully as if it has happened. Then extend it to six months and see what else you could add. Then follow the same process and go to 1 year, 2 years, 5 years, 10 years and finally 20 years. In 90 seconds it is just about getting a feel for each one; you do not have to be too specific or spend too much time on each stage. Make sure you smile and experience each new stage fully.

Make sure you follow your exercise preparation routine and understand the instructions. If not, read everything again and BEGIN!

30 seconds after exercise: Now close your eyes and imagine having what you feel now stay with you when you talk to friends, students, teachers, parents and anyone else you spend time with today. If completing charity component, know that you becoming happier is also raising money to help others too. Imagine how they must feel to know you're helping them as well.

After Challenge 9

On a scale of 1-10, how happy am I feeling?

(1 = very unhappy and 10 = extremely happy)

Score: _____

On a scale of 1-10, how stressed am I feeling?

(1 = very little and 10 = extremely stressed)

Score: _____

Optional Question 1: What did you like and/or dislike about this challenge?

_____

_____

_____

_____

Optional Question 2: Did you learn anything you could use in the future? If so, what?

_____

_____

_____

_____

Highest % Happiness Boost Recorded: 33% by 16-year-old male

Largest % Stress Decrease Recorded: 60% by 16-year-old female

Best Comment: Liked thinking about the future

Daily Happiness and Stress Measure before & after each Challenge

Name and/or Identification Number

_____

Date _____ Age _____ Gender _____

Name: Positivity Prompts

Before Challenge

On a scale of 1-10, how happy am I feeling?

(1 = very unhappy and 10 = extremely happy)

Score: _____

On a scale of 1-10, how stressed am I feeling?

(1 = very little and 10 = extremely stressed)

Score: _____

Challenge 10: Positivity Prompts

Present-focused exercise

Time: 90 seconds

Requirements: Several options explained below

Exercise Preparation: Sit or stand straight and begin breathing deeply. Close your eyes and focus on letting go of any particular worries, concerns or doubts you have. Perhaps imagine your thoughts evaporating. With each breath, feel centered, smile and promise yourself to commit fully to the challenge. Once committed, open your eyes, keep your smile, and continue to feel centered and breathing deeply.

Instructions: You are going to find and experience positive feelings prompted through another medium. You will find and use anything that has given you great feelings (inspirational, humorous, or entertaining) in the past to feel those feelings again. Options include reading a passage or page from your favorite book out loud, going to your picture collection, or finding a favorite video clip on a site like YouTube.

Rationale: The point of this exercise is that happy feeling prompts are around you constantly. All you need to do IS ACCESS THEM!

Process: You could also try this with something you haven't seen or read before, but that is riskier as you may not find it enjoyable. Of course, if you were to seek out an author or filmmaker who you usually like, that may work for you. Remember to fully engage in the experience, smile and enjoy it. If none of these things are available, you could also just do it through memory. Most people can easily enjoy reciting a favorite poem, lines or scenes from a movie or remembering certain great pictures, important jewelry or other symbolic and meaningful gifts.

Make sure you follow your exercise preparation routine and understand the instructions. If not, read everything again and BEGIN!

30 seconds after exercise: Now close your eyes and imagine having what you feel now stay with you when you talk to friends, students, teachers, parents and anyone else you spend time with today. If completing charity component, know that you becoming happier is also raising money to help others too. Imagine how they must feel to know you're helping them as well.

After Challenge 10

On a scale of 1-10, how happy am I feeling?

(1 = very unhappy and 10 = extremely happy)

Score: _____

On a scale of 1-10, how stressed am I feeling?

(1 = very little and 10 = extremely stressed)

Score: _____

Optional Question 1: What did you like and/or dislike about this challenge?

_____
_____
_____
_____

Optional Question 2: Did you learn anything you could use in the future? If so, what?

_____
_____
_____
_____

Highest % Happiness Boost Recorded: 33% by 13-year-old female

Largest % Stress Decrease Recorded: 100% by 13-year-old male

Best Comment: You can always think of the good things no matter what time nor what day it is. Thank you.

Daily Happiness and Stress Measure before & after each Challenge

Name and/or Identification Number

Date _____ Age _____ Gender _____

Name: Miracle Mirror

Before Challenge

On a scale of 1-10, how happy am I feeling?

(1 = very unhappy and 10 = extremely happy)

Score: _____

On a scale of 1-10, how stressed am I feeling?

(1 = very little and 10 = extremely stressed)

Score: _____

Challenge 11: Miracle Mirror

Present-focused exercise

Time: 60-90 seconds

Requirements: A mirror or good reflective surface

Exercise Preparation: Sit or stand straight and begin breathing deeply. Close your eyes and focus on letting go of any particular worries, concerns or doubts you have. Perhaps imagine your thoughts evaporating. With each breath, feel centered, smile and promise yourself to commit fully to the challenge. Once committed, open your eyes, keep your smile, and continue to feel centered and breathing deeply.

Instructions: You are going to smile fully and watch yourself doing it. The key to this exercise is to focus on the feeling of happiness in your face and not be critical about your appearance. If your focus shifts to your physical appearance, especially if they are negative judgments, let go of those thoughts and let them evaporate and bring your attention back to the feelings of happiness in your face.

Rationale: The point of this exercise is for you to make smiling and feeling good more natural and appreciate the POTENTIAL JOY AND ACCESSIBLE HAPPINESS THAT IS IN YOU!

Process: As you look in the mirror, your job is also to act in a way that will make a positive impression on the other person. Feel free to talk to them politely and give them compliments such as imagining or saying out loud (preferred) "you have a fantastic smile" and "you really are quite attractive" or whatever feels naturally positive.

Make sure you follow your exercise preparation routine and understand the instructions. If not, read everything again and BEGIN!

30 seconds after exercise: Now close your eyes and imagine having what you feel now stay with you when you talk to friends, students, teachers, parents and anyone else you spend time with today. If completing charity component, know that you becoming happier is also raising money to help others too. Imagine how they must feel to know you're helping them as well.

After Challenge 11

On a scale of 1-10, how happy am I feeling?

(1 = very unhappy and 10 = extremely happy)

Score: _____

On a scale of 1-10, how stressed am I feeling?

(1 = very little and 10 = extremely stressed)

Score: _____

Optional Question 1: What did you like and/or dislike about this challenge?

_____
_____
_____
_____

Optional Question 2: Did you learn anything you could use in the future? If so, what?

_____
_____
_____
_____

Highest % Happiness Boost Recorded: 29% by 13-year-old female

Largest % Stress Decrease Recorded: 33% by 13-year-old female

Best Comment (Teacher): Actually it was a lot of fun... It's ok to give yourself a little pep talk.

Daily Happiness and Stress Measure before & after each Challenge

Name and/or Identification Number

_____

Date _____ Age _____ Gender _____

Before Challenge

On a scale of 1-10, how happy am I feeling?

(1 = very unhappy and 10 = extremely happy)

Score: _____

On a scale of 1-10, how stressed am I feeling?

(1 = very little and 10 = extremely stressed)

Score: _____

Challenge 12: Gregarious Giving

Present-focused exercise

Time: 90 seconds

Requirements: Whatever you find that is applicable

Exercise Preparation: Sit or stand straight and begin breathing deeply. Close your eyes and focus on letting go of any particular worries, concerns or doubts you have. Perhaps imagine your thoughts evaporating. With each breath, feel centered, smile and promise yourself to commit fully to the challenge. Once committed, open your eyes, keep your smile, and continue to feel centered and breathing deeply.

Instructions: You are going to imagine giving away three things you currently have to three people you know in less than 90 seconds. This will be a race against the clock to think of the people you know, the things you have and what you will give of yours to that other person.

Rationale: The point of this exercise is for you to enjoy the process of quickly finding something of value for someone else and to experience the PLEASURE OF GIVING IT TO THEM.

Process: You could imagine giving any **low cost** thing away as long as it is something of potential value for the other person. It could be a book, movie, piece of art, music, food, jewelry, trinkets, cards, posters etc. If you have time, also imagine yourself actually giving it to them and them receiving it. They must be gifts of low cost that you are willing to give away, because you will.

Make sure you follow your exercise preparation routine and understand the instructions. If not, read everything again and BEGIN!

30 seconds after exercise: Now close your eyes and imagine having what you feel now stay with you when you talk to friends, students, teachers, parents and anyone else you spend time with today. If completing charity component, know that you becoming happier is also raising money to help others too. Imagine how they must feel to know you're helping them as well.

Extension: Next time you are with that person, give it to them and tell them why you wanted to give it to them.

After Challenge 12

On a scale of 1-10, how happy am I feeling?

(1 = very unhappy and 10 = extremely happy)

Score: _____

On a scale of 1-10, how stressed am I feeling?

(1 = very little and 10 = extremely stressed)

Score: _____

Optional Question 1: What did you like and/or dislike about this challenge?

_____

_____

_____

_____

Optional Question 2: Did you learn anything you could use in the future? If so, what?

_____

_____

_____

_____

Highest % Happiness Boost Recorded: 40% by 11-year-old male

Largest % Stress Decrease Recorded: 60% by 15-year-old male

Best Comment: Giving ✓ (drew a large tick)

Daily Happiness and Stress Measure before & after each Challenge

Name and/or Identification Number

_____

Date _____ Age _____ Gender _____

Name: Tantalizing Touch

Before Challenge

On a scale of 1-10, how happy am I feeling?

(1 = very unhappy and 10 = extremely happy)

Score: _____

On a scale of 1-10, how stressed am I feeling?

(1 = very little and 10 = extremely stressed)

Score: _____

Challenge 13: Tantalizing Touch

Present-focused exercise

Time: 90 seconds

Requirements: Whatever you find that is applicable

Exercise Preparation: Sit or stand straight and begin breathing deeply. Close your eyes and focus on letting go of any particular worries, concerns or doubts you have. Perhaps imagine your thoughts evaporating. With each breath, feel centered, smile and promise yourself to commit fully to the challenge. Once committed, open your eyes, keep your smile, and continue to feel centered and breathing deeply.

Instructions: This is a touch-based exercise and you do not need anything specific to be able to do it as you can touch whatever is around you. If you prefer, you may find something that has a particularly interesting feel to it. You could use a variety or hard and soft, hot and cold, e.g. a fluffy towel, a desk, hot water and ice. You are going to explore via touch any items you have with you or around you very slowly and enjoy the feel of them.

Rationale: The point of this exercise is that the enjoyment of TOUCHING IS AVAILABLE TO YOU AT ANYTIME WHEN DONE SLOWLY AND WITH APPRECIATION!

Process: Close your eyes and concentrate on using the very tips of your fingertips to touch the objects you have. Make sure you do it slowly, enjoy the sensations produced and smile.

Make sure you follow your exercise preparation routine and understand the instructions. If not, read everything again and BEGIN!

30 seconds after exercise: Now close your eyes and imagine having what you feel now stay with you when you talk to friends, students, teachers, parents and anyone else you spend time with today. If completing charity component, know that you becoming happier is also raising money to help others too. Imagine how they must feel to know you're helping them as well.

After Challenge 13

On a scale of 1-10, how happy am I feeling?

(1 = very unhappy and 10 = extremely happy)

Score: _____

On a scale of 1-10, how stressed am I feeling?

(1 = very little and 10 = extremely stressed)

Score: _____

Optional Question 1: What did you like and/or dislike about this challenge?

_____
_____
_____
_____

Optional Question 2: Did you learn anything you could use in the future? If so, what?

_____
_____
_____
_____

Highest % Happiness Boost Recorded: 20% by 12-year-old female

Largest % Stress Decrease Recorded: 100% by 13-year-old male

Best Comment (Teacher): The touching exercise actually helped me to focus and to clear my mind. Very useful, I will use this again.

Daily Happiness and Stress Measure before & after each Challenge

Name and/or Identification Number

_____

Date _____ Age _____ Gender _____

Name: Pleasure Piling

Before Challenge

On a scale of 1-10, how happy am I feeling?

(1 = very unhappy and 10 = extremely happy)

Score: _____

On a scale of 1-10, how stressed am I feeling?

(1 = very little and 10 = extremely stressed)

Score: _____

Challenge 14: Pleasure Piling

Past and/or Present-focused exercise

Time: 90 seconds

Requirements: Nothing.

Exercise Preparation: Sit or stand straight and begin breathing deeply. Close your eyes and focus on letting go of any particular worries, concerns or doubts you have. Perhaps imagine your thoughts evaporating. With each breath, feel centered, smile and promise yourself to commit fully to the challenge. Once committed, open your eyes, keep your smile, and continue to feel centered and breathing deeply.

Instructions: You will think of as many pleasurable experiences as you can. They can be anything that may have happened in the past, any enjoyable feelings or sensations you may have now or anything great that could happen in the future. There are no restrictions.

Rationale: The point of this exercise is that you CAN BE AND FEEL HAPPY ABOUT ANYTHING NOW!

Process: For example, it could be a previous kiss, recent kiss or future kiss. You could be a great experience of the past, a sensation of the present or an image of an incredible future. There are no limitations. You will simply spend 90 seconds imagining as many enjoyable things as possible. Close your eyes and with each pleasurable image or sensation that you feel, smile and imagine stacking it onto the last one so you build a mountain of pleasurable experiences one on top of the other as you notice and experience piling of the sights, sounds, smells, touches and tastes of each experience.

Make sure you follow your exercise preparation routine and understand the instructions. If not, read everything again and BEGIN!

30 seconds after exercise: Now close your eyes and imagine having what you feel now stay with you when you talk to friends, students, teachers, parents and anyone else you spend time with today. If completing charity component, know that you becoming happier is also raising money to help others too. Imagine how they must feel to know you're helping them as well.

After Challenge 14

On a scale of 1-10, how happy am I feeling?

(1 = very unhappy and 10 = extremely happy)

Score: _____

On a scale of 1-10, how stressed am I feeling?

(1 = very little and 10 = extremely stressed)

Score: _____

Optional Question 1: What did you like and/or dislike about this challenge?

_____

_____

_____

_____

Optional Question 2: Did you learn anything you could use in the future? If so, what?

_____

_____

_____

_____

Highest % Happiness Boost Recorded: 67% by 12-year-old female

Largest % Stress Decrease Recorded: 67% by 15-year-old male

Best Comment: I remembered all the happy things I forgot that had happened, so thank you.

Bonus Comment: You're da bomb! Sick ladd thx for making me happy (14 year-old-male)

MEASURE OF OVERALL HAPPINESS –
After Challenge - By Aleks George Srbinoski
May be re-printed for personal use only.

Name and/or Identification Number

_____

Date _____ Age _____ Gender _____

1. On average, how happy as a person am I?

(1 = very unhappy and 10 = extremely happy)

Score: _____

2. On average, how stressed do I feel each day?

(1 = very little and 10 = extremely stressed)

Score: _____

Bonus Week

First of all, congratulations on completing the challenge! As you may have discovered, some of the challenges were more enjoyable to you than others. That is why this additional week is so important.

In the bonus week, the goal is to do any challenge you want as often as you like. You are completely free! You can do the exact same exercise every day, or perhaps your top 2 or 3 over the week, or maybe your favorite 7. You can do them just once a day or more. It is up to you. For personal use only, you can print out previous score sheets to individually score yourself too. It is also fine if you choose not to score each individual exercise that you do over the week.

Each exercise is only 60-120 seconds, so play around and see what you like. Once the bonus week is over, I highly recommend you then make your favorite exercises a scheduled part of your daily life. Surely you can spare two minutes a day to develop happiness and reduce stress!

Feel free to contact me anytime and let me know how it goes.

To your happiness,

Aleks

<u>MEASURE OF OVERALL HAPPINESS –</u>
<u>After Bonus Week - By Aleks George Srbinoski</u>
<u>May be re-printed for personal use only</u>

Name and/or Identification Number

_____

Date _____ Age _____ Gender _____

1. On average, how happy as a person am I?

(1 = very unhappy and 10 = extremely happy)

Score: _____

2. On average, how stressed do I feel each day?

(1 = very little and 10 = extremely stressed)

Score: _____

Part 2

102 Happiness Tips

Are your children happier in their virtual world?

Researchers for UK-based children's charity Kidscape, assessed the online activities of 2,300 11-18 year-old's and reported that 45% said that they were "sometimes" happier online then in their real lives.

In their report, *Virtual life is more than a game, it is your life*, 47% of children said they act differently and feel more powerful and confident online.

These findings indicate that children could struggle to grow up with the necessary skills to handle real life. Here are my tips to raise happy children in the real world:

1. Increase communication. Discuss the pros and cons of the virtual versus the real world.

2. Monitor the time they spend online and highlight the dangers.

3. Encourage and schedule fun regular activities outside of the home.

You will be judged by your first impression

A study titled *Your Best Self Helps Reveal Your True Self* out of the University of British Columbia suggests that people who make an effort to create a positive and authentic first impression are judged by others as more normal and better liked.

Positive self-presenters were also judged more accurately in terms of their personality and IQ.

Here are my tips for making a positive first impression:

1. Create a relaxed and open body posture and keep your head up looking forward.

2. Look towards the other person's eyes and as soon as they meet your gaze – smile. Emotions are contagious. Your positive emotion is likely to lead them to feel the same way.

3. Express yourself passionately! You can stay within social norms and still enjoy talking about yourself and your interests in an exciting way.

Will the newly discovered happiness gene determine your destiny?

An article from the *Journal of Human Genetics* states that the gene 5-HTT is said to be responsible for how nerve cells distribute serotonin, nicknamed "the happiness drug," which is a chemical produced by the brain that controls mood.

The long version of the gene is reported to lead to more serotonin transportation and people with lower levels of serotonin are known to be more prone to depression

However, it is also stated that life experiences and psychological skills also play a large role in overall happiness and life success.

Here are three key points to take away from such a finding:

1. Genetics do play a part in happiness but are NOT the only factor. Your life experiences and psychological skills are also critical.

2. Focus on the things you can control. You cannot change your genes, but you can always work on improving your skills in any area of life.

3. Spend more time with positive people. Choose to surround yourself with happy and successful people and you too will naturally improve.

Find ways to reduce your stress today if you want to improve your health

Researchers at Mayo Clinic in Rochester claim that reducing worker stress is likely to be the best measure for improving employee health.

Mayo surveyed 13,198 workers and found highly stressed employees reported poorer quality of life, health, support and fatigue as well as having higher blood pressure, blood sugar, cholesterol. They were also more likely to be overweight.

In order to begin reducing your stress today, here are three quick tips:

1. Set aside at least 5-10 minutes each day in a quiet place to focus on breathing deeply and being relaxed.

2. Regularly schedule time for an activity that promotes calmness. This could be tai chi, yoga, meditation or walking in a peaceful area.

3. Take some time out to laugh and have fun. Meet with friends, play games, or watch a comedy. Commit to taking some time to enjoy the lighter side of life.

Could quitting work altogether make you happier?

Research from the Université de Montréal claims that people who do not work and who are not looking for a job are often less stressed and happier than many people who are employed.

One of the reasons for this is that those who work in stressful and unfulfilling environments often express negative emotions related to work at home.

Here are three quick tips to help you let go of work issues when returning home:

1. Before leaving work, spend a few minutes writing down all your current concerns and some ideas of how you can deal with them the next day.

2. Before you enter your home, spend up to a minute breathing deeply and focusing on letting go of current work issues.

3. As you breathe deeply, set up an internal expectation of being in a harmonious environment by imagining acting calmly at home.

Rise and shine and tweet. Is Twitter studying your happiness patterns?

Cornell University researchers analyzed the English language tweets of 2.4 million people in 84 countries over a 2-year period.

They used a computer program to search for words related to moods and found that in most cases, positive attitude peaks early in the morning and again close to midnight whilst mood dips in midmorning.

Here are three quick tips to help you take advantage of your mood related rhythms:

1. Use a notebook and give yourself a positive mood score between 1 and 10 every waking hour for a week.

2. Write a list of activities that boost your mood such as music, reading, sending an email to a good friend and so on.

3. During times of the day when your mood drops, consider taking a short break and utilizing one of your mood booster strategies.

At what price would you sell your happiness?

A study out of Cornell University suggests that the majority of people would take a high-paying job with longer work hours over a good-paying job with more reasonable demands on their time, and with feelings of greater happiness overall.

Researcher Rees-Jones suggests people make trade-offs between happiness and other things such as health, family happiness, social status and sense of purpose.

However, in my opinion, these are all aspects of true happiness.

Here are three questions to ask yourself in order to discover what actions will make you truly happy:

1. Will this decision allow me to feel proud when I look back on this decision 10 years from now?

2. Will this action I am taking be sustainable in the long term?

3. If my best friend was in this situation, what advice would I give him or her?

A wandering mind is an unhappy mind

A Harvard University study has shown that unhappy people often have a wandering mind.

Using 2,250 volunteers ranging from 18-88 and from a diverse range of backgrounds, the study found that those who spent less time engaged in the present moment by frequently thinking and worrying about other things were the least happy.

Here are three activities to consider pursuing. Each will train you to focus on being in the moment:

1. Meditation

2. Competitive games or sports that require quick decisions

3. Active socializing with a focus on fun, friendship and laughter

Can too much happiness crush your effectiveness?

A review of happiness research coauthored by assistant professor of psychology at Yale University, June Gruber, indicates that happiness can be detrimental in some contexts.

Findings suggest that happy people tend to think less concretely and systematically. They are also poor perceivers of threat.

However, it is important to remember that every emotion has a purpose and happiness should not be the desired state at all times.

Here are three questions to help you be happy and effective:

1. What is the best emotion to access based on what I am doing?

2. How can I efficiently complete or delegate tasks that don't make me feel happy?

3. Who can I get to help me when I am not confident in what I am doing?

The three killers of teenage happiness

Researchers at Xavier University in Cincinnati and Baylor University in Texas surveyed 1,329 high schoolers and found that teens who are materialistic and compulsive spenders, as well as teens who either have too much spare time or not enough spare time were linked with lower levels of happiness.

The researchers suggest that it is crucial that teenagers enjoy a sensible and balanced amount of free time that is not focused on consumer related behavior.

Here are three quick tips to help create happy and healthy teenagers:

1. Ask teens how they would ideally like to spend their free time and brainstorm fun activities for them to do.

2. Schedule in activities that are not consumption based like sports, games, walks and so on.

3. Give teens adequate time for rest and recuperation after busy times.

Can your Facebook picture reveal how happy you are?

Over two studies, psychologists from the University of Virginia found that men and women who flashed "intense" smiles in their first-semester Facebook profile photos reported having greater life satisfaction than those who did not.

In addition to this, those same students were likelier to report high levels of contentedness during their last semester of university, a full 3 1/2 years later.

Study co-author J. Patrick Seder claims the findings are noteworthy because they are based on informally shot photos and their research supports previous findings where formal portraits were used.

Here are three quick tips to increase the frequency of your intense smiles:

1. Go play a game or two with some highly active children.

2. Watch an inspirational or comedic film or show.

3. Organize regular outings with the happiest people you know.

Is 38 the age of greatest happiness?

A survey of 2000 British adults conducted by The Huffington post U.K, indicated that 38 is the age when people are the most happy and content in life.

An additional finding was that older respondents tended to suggest that happiness reached its peak at 48. Site editor Georgia James stated that these findings show how age and experience can provide a wealth of benefits.

Here are three tips to being happy at any age:

1. Reflect on how you continue to learn as you age. Consider what you know now in comparison to 10 years ago.

2. Focus on your strengths and on the areas of life where you can continue to develop as you age.

3. Regularly review the activities that make you happy and do your best to maintain or appropriately modify those activities as you age.

Is happiness the #1 predictor of long life?

A research team led by Andrew Steptoe from the University College London who surveyed 3,800 individuals between the ages of 52 and 79 claim that older people who feel content, excited or happy on a typical day have a 35% smaller chance of dying.

These findings tended to hold true, even after taking into account the participants physical health, mental health and financial situation.

Here are three quick ways to increase excitement, contentment and happiness during your day:

1. Send a quick text, email or note to a friend about anything that is positive.

2. Take a minute to close your eyes and recall a time when you felt calm and content and re-experience it again by immersing yourself in that memory.

3. Take a minute to close your eyes and become excited about an enjoyable event that is likely to occur in your future such as a holiday, event or receiving a gift.

IPhone app says sex, exercise and the arts make us happiest

A British iPhone survey has found that second to sex and exercise, viewing or participating in a range of arts related activities, like theatre, performance, museums and crafts, lead to the highest levels of reported happiness.

Using the Mappiness app, more than 46,000 participants entered information about what made them happy at random intervals with over 3 million answers being recorded.

Here are three tips to help you find and enjoy your creative side:

1. Consider which of the arts you enjoy the most (e.g. museums, theatre, concerts, crafts) and schedule time to enjoy them at least once a month.

2. Surround yourself with creative people by joining an arts related club or society.

3. Make or offer arts related gifts for people that everyone can enjoy.

Moderate exercise is found to improve sleep and mental health

A study from the *Journal of Mental Health and Physical Activity* has found that people who spend at least 150 minutes a week on moderate to vigorous activity sleep up to 65% better than those who do not. They also feel more productive and focused during the day.

These findings suggest regular physical activity may serve as a non-pharmaceutical alternative to improving sleep and increasing overall well-being.

Here are three simple ways to increase moderate activity during the week:

1. Walk, cycle or park your car at least 10 minutes away from your workplace.

2. Schedule more outdoor activities with the entire family and bring a ball to family picnics.

3. Whenever possible, maintain a regular routine by choosing the exact same time of day to exercise.

Are their times when happiness truisms are wrong?

A research article titled *Beyond Positive Psychology* has given specific examples of contradictions in classic happiness findings.

Forgiveness can be damaging for people who remain in abusive relationships, optimism can cause people to ignore obvious problems with intimate relationships and sometimes unkindness is called for during difficult times in a relationship.

Knowing that not every rule can fit every situation, here are three questions to consider when a positive response is usually expected:

1. Can I forgive this person without losing my self-respect?

2. Am I being overly optimistic and not looking at this situation realistically?

3. Am I using kindness or other positive actions or emotions as an excuse to avoid confronting the real issue?

Regular sex found to be a major key to happiness for older married couples

The *Gerontological Society of America* surveyed 238 couples aged 65 or older and found that the frequency of sexual activity often predicted general well-being.

For those who reported no sexual activity in the past year, only 40% said they were "very happy with life," whilst for those who engaged in sexual activity more than once a month, 60% said they were "very happy with life" and 80% of those said they were "very content" in their marriage.

Knowing that sex is important at any adult age, here are three tips to increase the chances of remaining sexually active as you age:

1. Refuse to entertain limiting beliefs or stereotypes about age. Work to maintain a positive attitude towards sex throughout life.

2. Maintain regular physical activity and focus on a healthy diet designed to prevent or maintain chronic health conditions from worsening.

3. Seek professional assistance if major changes in libido occur. Sex related programs, techniques and medical treatments continue to advance and should be investigated if warranted.

Small acts of kindness will create a happy marriage

Rather than focusing only on expensive gifts and trips, it appears that the secret to a happy marriage is concentrating on the little things.

Giving your spouse a back rub, making the bed and offering a cup of tea are all small acts with great cumulative effects according to a recent study on marital generosity by the University of Virginia.

After sexual satisfaction and sense of commitment, acts of generosity appear to be essential requirements for maintaining a healthy long-term relationship.

Here are three tips to create and maintain a generous and harmonious relationship:

1. Ask yourself what is one small thing I could do for my partner on a regular basis that I know they would appreciate.

2. Offer regular praise. Whenever you notice your partner doing something you like, thank them for it.

3. Use fun regular reminders if you plan to offer a larger gift. For example, if you're going on a holiday, bring a brochure home or get your partner a book, movie or other gift about where you are going.

Are older people the happiest in society?

Finding the reasons why it appears that people become happier as they age is the focus of an article by psychologist Derek M. Isaacowitz and the late Fredda Blanchard-Fields.

Previous research has indicated that older people recall happier memories when looking at pictures of faces and varying situations and more frequently prune negative people from their life.

However, the reasons for this are yet to be conclusively determined.

Despite still being uncertain as to why the link between happiness and age exists, we can still practice utilizing the same happiness bias principles.

Here are three ways to do that:

1. Create a photo album with pictures that lead you to recall your happiest memories.

2. When facing ambiguous situations, spend some time imagining and considering how you could create a positive outcome.

3. Schedule more time with positive friends and reduce or even eliminate the time you spend with negative people.

Are simple acts essential for happiness?

According to the *Feel Good Factor Index* which was created through surveying 2,014 British people, the simple things in life such as smiles and walks make people happiest.

Although the acts most likely to increase happiness include spending time with family and enjoying the achievements of loved ones, 27% of respondents said having someone "be nice or smile at me" and 24% said "taking a walk on a beautiful day" make them feel happier.

Here are three tips to increase the amount of simple positive acts in your day:

1. Set a goal to smile and compliment at least three people each day. Often they will return the favor.

2. Schedule in time for a short walk during the nicest part of the day.

3. Don't just rely on others. Remember to compliment and praise yourself with a smile and some encouraging words or thoughts whenever you complete a positive act.

Can working too much in a job you find satisfying still lead to depression?

The Finnish Institute of Occupational Health and the University College London followed 2,000 middle aged British civil servants for close to six years. They found that even in workers with no previous mental illness issues and who are satisfied and supported at work, major depression was still likely to occur for excessive overtime workers.

The rate of major depressive episodes were 2.43 times higher for those who worked more than 11 hours a day compared with employees who worked 7-8 hours a day.

Here are three tips to help you reduce your work hours:

1. To be more effective, take a short 5-10 minute break every 30-60 minutes. During that time eat something healthy, stay hydrated and practice a short deep breathing or other relaxation exercise.

2. Create a distraction-free environment to complete your most demanding tasks.

3. Complete your most important tasks as early as possible in the day.

Could living alone make you happier?

Eric Klinenberg, Professor of Sociology at New York University, conducted more than 300 in-depth interviews and found that in comparison to co-habitators, people who live alone are more likely to exercise, eat out, volunteer and attend extracurricular classes, public events and lectures.

Klinenberg stated that although single life can be lonely, it can also help people discover new things about themselves and appreciate the pleasure of good company.

Whether single or co-habitating here are three tips to help you enjoy life:

1. Do not let the lack of company or a training partner stop you from exercising regularly.

2. Always aim to expand your social circle.

3. Eat out with a group of people whenever possible. Of course, still stick to your budget and dietary goals when you do this.

Online role-playing games are killing marital happiness

Recent findings are confirming the common perception that online role-playing games often interfere with real-world relationships.

A survey conducted by researchers at Brigham Young University has found that ¾ of spouses of online gamers wished their partners put more time and effort into their marriages and less on their avatars.

The main issues were resulting arguments, disrupted bedtime routines and less time spent on shared activities or engaging in serious conversation.

Here are three guidelines to follow if you or your partner is an online gamer:

1. Set specific scheduled times for gaming and maintain them.

2. As long as rule #1 is followed, seek to understand and maintain a positive attitude towards your partner's gaming.

3. Endeavor to spend at least one night a week where gaming would usually occur on a new activity that both people can enjoy.

Good intentions lead to happy times

The University of Maryland Mind Perception and Morality Lab has conducted mind probing studies suggesting that although what you do is important, why you do something (your intent) is actually much more important in determining what shapes the quality of your life and the lives of people around you.

As long as your intent is positive, your mistakes will often result in less severe consequences.

For example, stomping on someone's foot results in less pain for the victim if he or she knows it is unintentional.

Here are three tips to spreading good intentions:

1. State your intention. Actually tell people what you are trying to do, especially when things do not go well.

2. Ask others what their intentions are to avoid miscommunication.

3. Assume positive intent when interacting with others. This will often lead to positive outcomes.

Youth depression is being predicted through Facebook status updates

Research by the University of Washington showed that 30% of the 200 Facebook-using student participants posted updates that met clinical depression symptoms criteria such as feelings of worthlessness, hopelessness, insomnia, over sleeping and reduced concentration.

Although it is hard to know which updates are serious, these findings suggest that a clinical screening may be very important for people demonstrating such symptoms.

Here are three tips to help you care for your friends online:

1. Look for a consistent pattern of difficulties over 1 to 2 weeks. A bad night's sleep may be ignored whilst a week of troubled sleep should not be.

2. If you notice a particular symptom that seems related to depression, ask them how else they have been feeling and functioning at work of late.

3. If concerned, offer to talk to them privately. If a close friend, simply call them and recommend they visit their family physician for a checkup.

Tragic movies can make you feel happier

A study published in *Communication Research* had 361 college students watch an abridged version of the 2007 movie tragedy *Atonement*. Participant emotions were measured before, during and after the screening and asked to rate how much they enjoyed the film and to write on how it reflected on themselves, their goals, their relationships and their lives in general.

Findings suggested the more viewers thought about their own loved ones when watching, the greater their increase in happiness afterwards as they tend to feel fortunate in comparison to the ordeals of the characters on screen.

Here are three tips to enjoying tragic stories:

1. After watching a sad movie or play, consider how what you saw can lead you to feel grateful for what you have.

2. After saddening experiences, write down three life lessons you learnt and how you could apply them.

3. Amplify the learnings by discussing with friends what you learnt and felt grateful for after watching sad movies and ask them to reciprocate.

Happiness is now on the global agenda

The United Nations implemented Resolution 65/309 which now places "happiness" on the global agenda.

Acknowledging that the pursuit of happiness is a fundamental human goal and that Gross Domestic Product is not the best indicator for a nation's prosperity, the resolution is a landmark step towards adopting a global-sustainability based economic paradigm that considers human happiness and well-being and not just economics as important measures of progress.

With that in mind, here are three areas where you could seek ways to make life happier:

1. Have a family dinner and get each member to offer methods for increasing family happiness.

2. Ask your colleagues at work what could be implemented at an organizational level to increase happiness.

3. Take some quiet time out for yourself and consider what changes to your activities and routines you could make to create a happier personal life.

Can too much happiness cost you money?

Research by Ed Diener, renowned for his investigations in happiness, analyzed a variety of studies, including data from more than 16,000 people around the world, and discovered that those who were happiest and most satisfied with life when younger tended to earn slightly less as adults than those slightly less merry when younger.

He explains that those who do not experience much sadness or anxiety are rarely dissatisfied with their jobs and feel less pressure to change careers or seek more education.

With that in mind, here are three important questions to ask yourself in order to use happiness as a motivator to maximizing your career:

1. If I was to improve my education, what would I really enjoy doing?

2. What types of work would I love to do that utilize my strengths and would energize me?

3. What kind of environmental changes can I make to grow my happiness and motivation?

Listen to music daily to improve your health and happiness

A doctoral thesis in psychology from the University of Gothenburg utilized a survey study of 207 individuals where one group of participants listened to self-chosen music for 30 minutes a day for 2 weeks and the other relaxed with no music.

Results indicated that positive emotions were experienced more often and more intensively. Likewise, they experienced less perceived stress and lower levels of stress hormones in connection to music listening.

Here are three tips to maximize the positive effect of music:

1. For the best effects, listen to the musical pieces that you love the most.

2. Create a folder with your favorite pieces around themes of interest, e.g. motivation, relaxation, inspiration, fun and so on.

3. Listen to non-distracting music to increase enjoyment when having to do menial tasks like washing dishes.

Become happier by changing your personality

Psychologists from The University of Manchester and London School of Economics and Political Science suggest that personalities can and do change over time which had been considered improbable until recently. Making empowering changes can increase well-being.

Findings lead researchers to conclude that fostering the conditions for personality growth through positive schooling, communities and parenting may lead to increased well-being and Gross Domestic Product growth.

Here are three tips to create an empowering personality:

1. Look for positive role-models and model applicable aspects of their behavior.

2. Spend as much time as possible with people you admire and who inspire you.

3. Schedule more activities in your life that cultivate the parts of your personality that you like the most.

Will talking about yourself make you happier?

A Harvard University study suggests that talking about yourself whether in person or through social media sites activates the reward centers of the brain and creates pleasurable affects similar to the effects created when we receive money or eat chocolate.

During the experiment many participants even forego money in order to disclose information about themselves indicating that we have a pleasure-based bias towards our own personal interests.

Based on these findings, here are three ways to improve your relationships:

1. In order to build rapport with others, ask them about themselves and their interests and get them to elaborate on the pieces of information you find the most compelling.

2. Find a common interest with your audience before talking about yourself in relation to it.

3. Speak about your interests passionately. Emotions are contagious. Even if your audience is not interested in what you have to say, when you express yourself passionately, they will often engage in the material anyway because they enjoy your company.

Could earning less than your peers increase your happiness?

According to research from the University of St Andrews, earning less than your peers could actually raise your life satisfaction, but only if you're under 45.

Rather than becoming jealous, younger workers felt incentivized, believing that they too could one day earn the same.

Unfortunately, this tends to harm the self-esteem of older employees because of beliefs around limited career opportunities.

Regardless of your age, here are three ways to use the success of others to fuel your own:

1. Analyze what more successful people are doing differently from you and incorporate the most useful things that they do into your own work.

2. Continually seek inspiration, wisdom and opportunity from role-models who became successful in their later years. There are plenty of examples of people like this.

3. Take a balanced view. Do not compare yourself to others based solely on income. Consider what other strengths you have that are of great value and also build on them as you age.

Does being ethical lead to happiness?

Using data from the 2005-06 World Values Survey, which asked hundreds of thousands of people in over 80 countries about their values, beliefs and happiness, Harvey James from the University of Missouri examined the survey responses of US, Canadian, Mexican and Brazilian citizens and found that participants who felt it was not acceptable to cheat on taxes or accept bribes were more satisfied with life.

He said that such actions allow people to feel good about themselves and avoid feelings of guilt and shame.

Here are three quick questions you can ask to help you make ethical decisions:

1. Which action is most likely to benefit myself and others?

2. What negative emotions will I have to face or be able to avoid in the long term by acting this way?

3. How can I ensure that my actions support my highest values?

Keys to lasting happiness

A study out of the University of California Riverside surveyed 481 people about their happiness.

Six weeks later participants were asked to identify a recent positive change in their life that made them happier. Six weeks after that, psychologists evaluated whether the happiness change had lasted.

Although it had for some, for most it did not and the reason appears to be because they either kept wanting more or because they stopped having positive experiences of the change.

However, those who could appreciate what they had and not want more too soon as well as continue seeking new positive life experiences maintained their happiness boost.

Based on this research, here are three ways to maintain happiness:

1. Practice being grateful. Spend a full week writing down what you are grateful for each day.

2. Do not expect the power of a positive event to continually fuel you. Aim to seek new positive experiences on a regular basis.

3. Take daily action steps towards your most inspiring tasks. Meaningful activity completion is the most effective way to feel happy at the end of the day.

Part 3

Short Happiness Articles

How to find inner peace – Learning to slow your racing mind

Smart Alek: Sometimes I just can't get my mind to stop racing.

Aleks Psych: (Sarcastically) Wow, how surprising.

Smart Alek: So many brilliant ideas, I wonder which ones should I follow through on?

Aleks Psych: You mean like the idea of cross fertilizing a cactus with poison ivy or making sandals out of banana skins.

Smart Alek: Yes, to name a couple. Those and many, many more.

Aleks Psych: Sometimes it is best to let your ideas stay as such.

Learning how to find inner peace requires knowing what to do to slow down our incredibly active minds. Why do we find ourselves thinking about a range of issues and possible scenarios, even when we do not want to? Our mind is always processing information in order to protect us. We need to know what the things around us mean and how we should respond to them. We need to make sense of our world in order to feel safe.

However, at any one time, there is a lot going on! Sometimes our minds become too active and we become overly stressed or even overwhelmed. At this point what we usually would like more than anything is an opportunity to quickly create an inner peace meditation in order to allow for a break from all the mind racing activity. In other words, learning how to find inner peace requires us to know how to take a break from ourselves.

As we experience our world, we create judgments about what things mean. These judgments are known as labels and they influence how we feel. The labels we most often use are either positive or negative. Something is either good or bad, ugly or beautiful, successful or stupid, rich or poor, comfortable or irritating and so on. However, to give yourself a break from yourself, you must understand how to find inner peace by seeking neutrality.

One way to find neutrality is to shift your mind from labeling to describing. Descriptions have no major feelings attached to them and by describing our current experiences our racing mind has to slow down and re-focus on the present moment allowing us to find a greater sense of peace. A description is something that is hard, or soft, tingly, sharp, dull, black, red, pungent, loud, bitter, sweet, flowing, still and so on.

How to find inner peace - Exercise: Consider this exercise next time your mind is racing and you feel the need to find neutral again. First, sit up straight with your head forward and breathe deeply. From that position, scan your environment using any of your five senses and describe what you are doing and sensing without any judgment. Although you can do this mentally, if possible, it is preferable to describe your experience out loud. An example might look like 'I see a black table; it is hard and has four silver legs. There is a throb in my head and a tingle in my lower back. I hear a computer humming. I can smell lavender. I am sinking further into my chair. There is a long black shadow across the door. I hear car horns and feel a tingling breeze against my neck. I just grabbed a bottle of water; the liquid is cool and bubbly. I take a sip and it slides down my throat' and so on.

Try this exercise for 3-5 minutes 1-2 times a day over the next week when you feel you need to find inner peace by resting your overactive mind. You might be surprised by how enjoyable finding neutral in a time of stress can be.

Emotion and psychology - The secret of true attractiveness

Smart Alek: I can't believe just how attractive I am!

Aleks Psych: Neither can I.

Emotion and psychology, rather than physical appearance, is the secret to attractiveness. This is because the physical world is illusory. What we perceive is rarely an accurate representation of the way things really are. Popular singers often mime, many people pretend to be wealthy but are debt ridden, and I am yet to find a magazine cover that has not been photo shopped.

Living in such an illusory world, it is understandable why many people feel like they can never measure up. That is because the reality is that they cannot measure up. Maybe this is why so many reality shows are now based on showcasing and promoting human weaknesses. People know they can not measure up to the usual media illusions of perfection and so feel better about themselves when they see other people acting poorly. Both of these extremes are addictive to watch, but neither genuinely attractive.

The biggest mistake I see many people make is neglecting the development of their emotion and psychology when attempting to become more attractive. Instead, they overly focus on physical appearance. Working on your appearance is fine, but it is not the key to attractiveness.

The key to attractiveness both in the social and the possible intimate sense is related to how often you display positive emotions. The emotions you spend the majority of your time living in will be the most influential factor in regards to how socially and physically attractive you are to yourself and other people.

I do not care how physically attractive someone is, if they consistently over time display strong negative emotions, they will become less attractive to other people. Think of a really attractive person. You can think of me if you like--don't worry I'm joking, or am I? If you had to choose between an extremely attractive but highly angry and depressive partner, or a moderately attractive but highly generous, joyful, fun, and happy partner, I guarantee you would eventually want the happy one. At first you may choose the extremely attractive person, but over time their emotion and psychology will lead you to see their true attractiveness, which is related to their consistent emotional displays and beliefs based on their psychology.

One thing researchers have consistently found is that one of the strongest predictors of happiness for people is having a fun, social and outgoing nature. This is what the positive psychology practitioners call being extroverted and gregarious. The reason for this is because we loop onto each other's emotions and so bringing a happy attitude to a social encounter will then be enhanced and amplified by other people's happy reactions to you. As the conversation continues, the positive emotion and psychology between the two people is amplified.

There are numerous accounts and evidence to support that emotion and psychology is the key to attractiveness. I'm always hearing about people who had surgery on their face to look more physically attractive at the cost of positive emotional expression. The Barbie doll Botox look--it often leads to the breakdown of intimate and social relationships. The stupidest thing you could ever do is make it difficult for you to be able to smile. This is for three reasons. Number 1, when you smile, you feel better. Number 2, when you smile, other people feel better. Number 3, nothing is more attractive in the social and long term intimate sense than a genuine smile.

Emotion and Psychology - Exercise: Choose at least three upcoming social encounters. Commit to enter into that encounter with as much positive emotion as you can and notice how the other person responds to you. If you are highly positive around people who are not used to seeing you that way, they may act surprised and be weary of your sudden increase in positive emotion. However, unless you picked a completely inappropriate time to express positive emotion (e.g. a funeral, a conflict, or confrontation with someone very angry), they will attune to you and more than likely begin to smile.

Building high self-esteem requires a more intelligent perspective.

Muhammad Alek: Success is simple. Less excuses and greater effort equals more success.

Aleksandar the Grateful: Utilizing, acknowledging and appreciating the efforts of others will also help.

Building high self-esteem is one of the key jobs of positive psychology practitioners. In my line of work, I often come across stressed students, erratic employees and burnt out business people. One of the common themes I see in such people is that they are too critical of themselves and frequently judge themselves harshly in comparison to others. I know that building high self-esteem in such people will require me to recognize a range of low self-esteem signs, such as beliefs of inadequacy, and teach them how to overcome fear of failure.

Do you know a person who often feels inadequate in comparison to other people because those other people never have to try as hard as them, and yet they always seem to do better than them? Now let me assume that that person at times is you. Part of these inadequate feelings may be due to your negative perception of yourself and they don't actually always do better than you. Let's say for argument's sake that they do. You are completely accurate about this scenario. What is likely to happen?

You beat yourself down. You say things like 'I'm not smart enough, if I was smarter than I would be able to learn it quicker and produce better results.' Some will even go so far as to say 'I am a failure because I didn't produce a grade or result as high as this person.' And, you know what, you're right. You are a failure! A failure in regards to how you are looking at the situation.

Let's take a different perspective. You have worked twice as hard as this other person and your grade or result was a little bit less. Now, if you gave everything you got and produced a great result for you, and they didn't try very hard at all and they obtained a reasonable result in comparison to what they could get, who should be more proud?

Who do you respect more in this scenario? If the person who has to work harder has the right attitude, they will actually enjoy the process more than the other person. While the other person is bored, as you reach your potential you are much more likely to move into states of flow which is where you become enjoyably engrossed in the activity.

Building high self-esteem requires developing the correct perspective. I believe that the most important factor is learning how to focus on your effort, not success. With continued effort, your own individual success will increase. If you are focused on success without a true understanding of effort, then you will fail.

Furthermore, this is only one side of the coin. This person has more ability than you in this particular area, but there are other areas where you will have more ability than them. During my studies, I was surrounded by brilliant people with much greater strengths in certain areas than I. Rather than feel inadequate; I would use the opportunity to learn. Rather than be disdainful of those kinds of people, I would be respectful and create friendships so I could learn from them. (Though I do admit, that at times, those kind of people can be very, very annoying, especially if they boast about not needing to try.) By learning from them, they would pull me up with them.

My results would improve, I wouldn't go as high as they would, but I would go higher than I could before. I would genuinely ask about their skills (their brilliance) and thank them for sharing some of their insights with me. That being said, what about the ways I (or you) may have helped others? A lot of the contributions I made did not increase any of my marks. I was good at using metaphors, simplifying ideas and concepts, helping others feel more confident and less burnt out, joking and playing at times.

Out of all these things, none of them were assessable or gradable in an objective sense. There was no test telling me how important any of these attributes were! However, I know that these factors are incredibly important and I know that you too have incredible talents, though not measurable or recognized, are essential for building high self-esteem.

Building High Self Esteem - Exercise: Make a list of all the ways you add to your personal or professional worlds that often go unacknowledged. Also write out a list of areas that you can continue to improve in and what advice or training you could seek in order to assist in those areas. Then choose the area that you feel you could benefit the most from improving and seek the required assistance.

Positive emotion and psychology building

Muhammad Alek: I influence others by becoming a tsunami of passion.

Aleksandar the Grateful: I influence others by remaining an immovable mountain.

Aleks Psych: I influence others through undivided empathic attention.

Smart Alek: I influence others through my unchallengeable wisdom.

In an interaction, whether it is one-on-one, or in a group, whoever displays the strongest emotion is leading the interaction at that point in time and influences the emotion and psychology of all the other people involved.

Therefore, in a two-person interaction, if one person is showing deep sadness and the other person is moderately joyful, the sad person will have a greater influence over the interaction at least in the beginning and will bring the emotion of the joyful person down towards sadness. Now, this is not necessarily a bad thing if the joyful person understands that he or she can still positively influence the emotion and psychology of the other person.

By coming down to that person's emotion, the joyful person has a better opportunity to understand and empathize. As a result of this, the sad person may begin to feel better and as the sad person begins to feel better the joyful person may then begin to take the lead and bring the emotion and psychology of the sad person up towards a more positive feeling.

Humans are social creatures and the more positive our social interactions the better we feel. In our brain we have what neuroscientists call mirror neurons. Basically, they help us tune into and copy the emotion of someone else so we can better understand them. As we do that, we loop with each other's emotion and the emotion builds in intensity. We also often then speak of similar ideas and concepts.

People often unconsciously reduce the intensity of their positive emotion and psychology in order to attune with the negative emotions of someone who has a higher status. However, it is not your status but the strength of the emotion you choose to generate that will determine your own moods and how you influence others.

Even if have a supervisor is often angry or stressed, it does not have to influence your mood. In an interaction with him or her, if you displayed an even stronger level of calm or excitement, you would be likely to influence them and reduce the intensity of their emotion even though they have the higher status.

Unfortunately though, this is rare, as most people unconsciously attune to the emotion and psychology states of the person with the higher status, rather than deciding to empathize with the person if it is possible and then lead them to a more positive emotion. At any point in an interaction, you are either leading or being led. If you are being led, make sure it is towards an emotional place you are willing to go.

Furthermore, you won't always have time to empathize with someone's emotion and psychology state and may simply need to choose to immediately influence the other person towards your emotion. Influence is not only important one-on-one but also in group situations.

Let me use an example of influence at the group level. I will use the example of a fire. If there is a fire, naturally because there is danger, everyone is going to feel fear. If one person begins to panic, everyone else's level of fear is going to increase as the panicking person is leading the group with the strongest emotion. In this situation, panic is going to equal disaster as when you are gripped with a negative emotion you cannot think clearly.

In order to avert disaster, a member of the group needs to generate an even more intense positive emotion such as confidence or determination and lead the group. The new emotional leader would need to show the panicking person and the rest of the group that they are intensely confident and will now be leading the group. This will then reduce the level of fear in the group and increase confidence as the group attunes to the new leader.

This, of course, will not eliminate the fear, as fear is an appropriate emotion in this situation. The confident leader will also still be afraid; it is just that they have decided to become even more intensely confident and determined to find safety. That is why, in order to lead others, the higher-status fire-fighter must manage his or her own fear and maintain confidence. If the fire-fighter begins to panic, unless someone else is somehow able to generate an even stronger level of a positive emotion, the group is likely to have no chance of averting disaster.

So, if the stronger emotion leads the interaction, the emotions you consistently and intensely generate is going to influence how others perceive and respond to you. If you are happy, other people around you will become happier. If you are generous, other people around you will become more generous, and if you are irritable other people around you will become more irritable as they naturally attune to your emotional leadership.

That is why in the long term, consistently happy people begin to maintain relationships with other consistently happy people and consistently sad people maintain relationships with other consistently sad people, or not at all because others are finding it hard to relate to them. I'm sure at some point in your life you have been to a party. Who is more influential? Who do you want to speak to more—the smiling bubbly person at the center of it all or the angry person in the corner? Out of those two people, who would you rather be?

Positive Emotion and Psychology Building: - Exercise: Choose one person you know and before your next encounter, consciously decide how you want to influence them. Decide on how you want them to feel during and after your encounter? Happy, confident, proud, comfortable, grateful etc. Write down what would you have to say and how you would have to act in order to achieve this outcome. If they are the kind of person that often speaks about problems, think of ways of changing the subject quickly towards more positive endeavors. Make sure you prepare yourself and commit to the outcome before the encounter and take emotional leadership (with a big genuine smile) as soon as you see them.

Celebrating your strengths and weaknesses

Aleks Psych: I know my strengths and I work on enhancing them every day.

Smart Alek: I know your weaknesses and I work on reminding you of them every day.

One of the key practices recommended by positive psychology practitioners is the importance of incorporating as many of your strengths into as many of your activities as possible. By doing this, you will significantly increase your chances of thoroughly enjoying those activities. However, I believe happiness is not always about your successes. When it comes to individual psychology, what makes people happy above all else is their attitude!

When was the last time you took on a task that you knew you would be very poor at, and decided to embrace it anyway? People are so terrified of experiencing things at which they know they will not be great. Having that attitude sets you back for two reasons.

The first is: how do you really know how you will do until you give it a good honest try? Secondly, you may be robbing yourself of a really enjoyable experience. It can be one of the hardest things in the world to do. If you can leave your self-criticism behind, you may find that pleasure is not only reserved for those in the A league, but happiness is also obtainable in the Z league.

I love visual arts. In my mind I have incredible images and ideas. There is only one small issue. I am a very, very, very poor visual artist. A pirate with a hook for a hand would do better than I. Children laugh at my work! I stink so bad that skunks don't come within a 10 mile radius when I am painting. But, here is the beautiful part. What causes happiness for me is that I don't care!

Why not embrace your suckiness? Who am I to deny my glorious right to produce aesthetically unrecognizable and insignificant work? Some of our happiest moments come in weakness. Falling over will always be funny. Home video bloopers will always exist and, I am sorry to say, but we have a biological drive to at times embarrass ourselves.

This too is part of the psychology of what makes people happy. This is how we learn to appreciate what we cannot do well and develop humility. Our weaknesses build the richness of life by allowing us to enjoy the brilliance of others without always feeling the need to compete. There are some challenges you cannot win, and that is fantastic!

Visual art was easily my worst subject in high school. I was so bad, I think my teacher tried to recommend that I stay away from the paint and stick to crayon. My charcoal sketches looked like they were created inside a mine and my pottery efforts never even came close to staying together, let alone surviving the kiln.

However, these experiences have not deterred me from my right to occasionally indulge in what I will call 'Outside of outsider abstract art' with my signature technique being referred to as Creative Rebellious Artistic Passion, or you can use the acronym if you prefer.

I spend the majority of my life working on and living towards my strengths which do lead to achieving true happiness. However, not every experience you have will cater to your strengths, nor should they. One way to build up your resistance against discomfort and possible adversity is to occasionally seek experiences where you know you will struggle.

I recently decided (not for the first time) to do some painting alongside my partner. While she painted a poignant portrait of me, I struggled to master a smiley face. Despite my abilities, we both had a wonderful time. She was impressed with my very minor progress and even suggested that I paint a portrait of her. I said, "I would love to but I value our relationship too much. Maybe later tonight before bed when you have your contact lenses out."

Celebrating your weaknesses - Exercise: Write down three activities at which you wish you could be great. Choose one and schedule at least a half hour period of time (preferably an hour or more) in the next month to indulge in the activity to the best of your ability. Try to leave your self-criticism behind and enjoy immersing yourself in the activity, enjoying the process rather than focusing on the outcome.

Empowering labels are essential

Aleks Psych: The labels you use will determine how happy you become.

Smart Alek: You are totally right. My favorites are Versace and Armani.

Aleks Psych: I am referring to the labels you use to describe yourself.

Smart Alek: You should have been more specific. I refer to myself as divine, regal and omnipotent.

Aleks Psych: You should also be more specific. You forgot delusional!

You must develop empowering labels. Labels are the basic words and ways people evaluate or judge experiences. We give ourselves and things labels all the time. Good, bad, ugly, exciting, failure, success, smart, dumb, poor, rich, beautiful, intelligent, weak, strong, selfish, cheap, giving, lost, stable, pathetic, horrible, amazing.

These are all labels we put on ourselves and others. The labels you use consistently shape the way you see yourself and the world. You need to be incredibly careful of the labels you use, because you learn to live towards such labels. They become self-fulfilling prophecies.

The labels we use become our triggers. If you are always calling yourself or someone you have a strong influence over stupid, then you or they will start to believe it. Even if you say you don't really mean it, words are powerful and we will unconsciously act in a way that is congruent with its meaning. It might be a subtle drop of the head, a change in breath, but it will have an effect.

Then your unconscious mind will access old memories of when you felt stupid and then interpret this event like the ones before it. This is because for whatever you look, you will find.

What if you used the word smart, would that have an effect? Absolutely, it will affect you in proportion to how much you believe it. You believe it a little, your body will change a little and you will feel a little better. If you believe it a lot, then you will have bigger effects. What if you're stuck in a particular mood and you really don't believe you are very smart at that point in time? Well, there are much better options then believing you are stupid.

It may be that you are a 'learner', or a 'novice' or 'human', or you may challenge with a phrase like 'a step closer to success,' or even a sentence like 'just because I make mistakes some of the time, it does not mean that I am completely stupid.' You see our labels often distort and influence too much of our reality. Stupid is a generalizing word that you look through it as if it applies to everything. But, no one could possibly be stupid or bad or a failure at everything that they do all of the time. Developing a positive vocabulary is what makes people happy.

Your labels need to be kind. You must have empowering labels that are still realistic. Beating yourself or other people down just sets everyone back several steps. They must be kind because your labels become part of your identity. Be very careful of the labels you accept, the labels you reject and your definition behind the labels you use.

Empowering labels - Exercise: Draw a vertical line down a blank page and on one side write down all your positive characteristics and on the other side what you consider to be your negative characteristics. Examine your positive characteristics and write down 1-3 extra actions you could do over the next week that would indicate to you that you are living by those qualities. Choose 1-3 of your negative characteristics and reframe them so they are more empowering in a similar fashion to the reframes of the 'stupid' example above. Then over the next week write down 1-3 actions you could do that would indicate to you that you are improving in this area (e.g. if you think you are stupid, create 1-3 actions that would indicate to you that you are at least reasonably smart some of the time.)

Gratitude thoughts are one answer to what causes happiness

Aleks Psych: Do you ever take the time to stop and appreciate all that you have?

Smart Alek: No! I prefer to take time to stop and whine about what I do not have.

Aleks Psych: Why is that?

Smart Alek: It is just so much easier.

Gratitude thoughts are one of many answers to what causes happiness. When it comes to life, there is one absolute guarantee. It is that you will face challenges. You will be pushed, prodded, afraid, stressed, saddened, angered, and heartbroken.

You will face and feel failure, rejection, vulnerability, criticism, and loneliness. There will be times where you feel life is too hard and you are too insignificant. You may fall into the horrible trap of negatively comparing yourself to others or ask debilitating questions like 'Why do I have all of these problems?'

Be aware that every thought has a counter thought, and every negative emotion is sending you a message about an issue that does have a solution. There are numerous strategies a person can use to overcome an issue. However, there is one activity that is a much better option than having to find a solution.

What if you could train yourself to have a continually evolving positive mindset? The majority of your challenges are not really challenges, but problems with your perspective. There are many tools used to create a positive mindset, but one of the most simple and effective is the daily practice of developing your gratitude thoughts.

How many people do you know (be sure to also consider yourself) who out of a day where ten or more positive events have occurred will dwell on the one or two criticisms or setbacks they faced. In fact, they will dwell on the criticisms or setbacks so much that they will struggle to remember even one of the positive events that had occurred.

By practicing the development of your gratitude thoughts on a daily basis, you will start to train yourself to be able to enjoy and recall more of the positive events that occur each day. It is also a very simple process. All that is required, is that you either at the time of the event, or later in the day, write down an experience that you enjoyed and feel grateful to have felt.

It could be anything! The feeling of a breeze, sunset, a kiss, a particular food, music, a show, receiving a smile, the beating of your heart, your ability to smell, solving a problem, whatever you like. You could even end up writing gratitude essays. Writing gratitude essays would intensify the process even more. Each time you do this, you are creating and strengthening new positive emotion generating pathways in your brain.

By noticing and appreciating some of the positive events that occur in your day, you will begin to understand the difference between optimism and pessimism and thus begin training yourself to develop a greater optimism towards life. One of the benefits of optimism is as your optimism increases you will find yourself being less affected by the power of negative events. You may also find that the negative events of your life do not occur as often as you once believed. There really are so many gratitude thoughts you could begin generating right now!

Creating gratitude thoughts and gratitude essays

Gratitude training - Exercise: Obtain a journal and for one week write down the first three things you remember about your day at the end of each day. At the end of the week, review what you have written and give yourself a happiness rating out of 10 for the week. Then in the second week, at the end of each day write down at least three things that you are grateful for (write down as many things as you can think of and do not worry if you repeat yourself on different days). After writing down each thing you are grateful for, spend a minimum of 30 seconds reliving that experience as vividly as possible in your mind. Then at the end of the week, give yourself a happiness rating for that week.

Compare the differences between the first and second week. If you enjoy the gratitude reliving process, continue to do it as often as you can, preferably every day. If you want to intensify the experience further, begin writing short gratitude essays at the end of each week summarizing and incorporating as many of your gratitude thoughts as possible.

Are religious people happier?

Muhammad Alek: Faith is about belief. As long as you keep an ethical and moral foundation, there is no set of beliefs more important than those that inspire self-belief.

Aleksandar the Grateful: Once you have strong self-beliefs, you must actively inspire others to do the same. Only when you do that, will you find what you are truly looking for.

The answer to the question are religious people happier is... maybe. There is no topic of discussion more dangerous than religion. This article is not about debating the existence of God, rather it is about celebrating the power of the human spirit regardless of whether someone is spiritual or religious or neither.

In my work as a psychologist, I meet all kinds of people, from all kinds of backgrounds and with all kinds of beliefs. I am extremely respectful of other people's beliefs but there is one belief (often religion based, but not always) that some people hold that neither I, nor any of the other credible positive psychology practitioners, can accept.

These are the people that claim that 100% or close to 100% of the responsibility of how their life is and will continue to be is due to external factors out of their control. One such example may be God. I have met people who pray every night for their life to change but actively do nothing to seek a real solution to the problems they face. I believe there is nothing wrong with having a belief in God, and to answer the great question, statistically speaking, the overall answer to this question is yes! I also have no problem with the idea that God may play a part in life events.

What I find concerning is when I meet people who have an over-reliance on God. These are the people that are dependent on God and use God as an excuse not to claim any responsibility for their past, current or future actions. Are these religious people happier? No! I believe that if you want to believe in God, believe in God as a guide and not a puppet-master.

To believe that you have no real influence over your life is incredibly disempowering in most cases. The research continually shows that those people that accept responsibility for their actions and in any event focus on what they believe they can control, regardless of other religious beliefs, are much healthier and happier.

If you think of great role-models, heroes of today, I am not aware of any who did not have a firm belief in the power of individual choice. That is what makes them heroic, because they made a choice to live and act a certain way.

In your life, there is one thing I can guarantee. You will face challenges. The challenges you face require analysis and acceptance of external uncontrollable factors. However, what is also required is for you to take responsibility and know that you always have options and that all choices carry consequences that will specifically increase or decrease the quality of your life.

Reflection Exercise: Think of three times in your life when you fell into the trap of completely blaming external factors for the challenges you faced. Looking back, knowing what you know now, write down what you could have done that would have created a more positive outcome (e.g. Perhaps it would have been specifically changing some of the actions you took or shifting your attitude towards the problem). Then consider how you will use these lessons to assist you in facing three possible future challenges.

Recreating causes of happiness

Muhammad Alek: Today, I am going to tear up a mountain. I will not stop until I reach the top.

Aleksandar the Grateful: As you catch your breath at the top, do not forget to remember the journey and appreciate the view.

Muhammad Alek: Then, I will race back down it.

Aleksandar the Grateful: As you catch your breath at the bottom, do not forget to remember the journey and appreciate the view.

In order to be living a fulfilling and happy life, it is important to seek new adventures and experiences that force you to learn and grow in order to develop the ability to meet the changing demands of life. Although moving forward is important in order to squeeze the juice out of living, reliving a past experience once in a while can also be highly enjoyable.

There is a reason why the action replay is so popular in sport. What causes happiness is a special experience that you are able to relive again and again and again. There are of course many other causes of happiness as well, and I will address these causes in other articles.

About twice a year, what causes happiness for me is creating the time to spend one to two hours returning to a much simpler time and life. Every six months or so, I return to one of my favorite activities as a teenager. I find my old games console, plug in the controller, uncover some old fighting games and get ready to find a feeling I can only describe as home. I dim the lights and look in my old CD cases in order to find the music that was my high school soundtrack.

Recently, I found myself in a very familiar role. I was the Japanese martial arts master Ryu taking on the evil Thai fighter Sagat in one of our epic battles while U2's Bono *Rattled and Hummed* about lost love, uncertainty, desire for new adventures and seeking of purpose. What causes happiness is the combination of me hitting a high note and creating the correct sequence in order to drive a winning fireball into my opponent, leading to exhilaration of victory.

Over the years friends have asked me why I have not gotten rid of that old games machine and bought an advanced one of today. I tell them that they are missing the point. What causes happiness in this situation is not the playing of video games. It is the reliving of the memories, emotions and associations connected to the experience.

Then there are other experiences that feel both old and new at the same time. Every year, on or around my birthday I hike up the main mountain of the city where I come from. As I move up it, I consider my life, how far I have come, the goals I have achieved and my future goals.

It is the same process each time. I hike up the mountain without stopping until I reach the top and find my own special rock. Feeling a strong sense of triumph, I sit on the rock and look out onto my childhood home and surrounding Pacific Ocean. I bask in the view, before closing my eyes to meditate for a short period. Then I rise and surf the forces of gravity by sprinting back down the mountain.

Each time I tackle that mountain I learn something new and relive great experiences of old. It is my sanctuary that I am committed to returning to at least once a year for many reasons, but one in particular. What causes happiness for me is a mountain. When I am on that mountain, I am happy. It is time to discover what causes happiness for you?

What causes happiness for you - Exercise: Think back to a time in your life when you felt very happy. Write down the enjoyable activities that you did. Then choose one and plan a way to relive that experience as fully as possible and schedule a time to do this within the next month. Afterwards consider writing what the old experiences that you felt were and what were the new experiences that came from the activity. If you enjoy it, consider regularly doing the activity every 6 to 12 months.

How to become a happy person - Develop quality relationships

Aleks Psych: Do you think we need to improve on the way we relate?

Smart Alek: No!

The secret of how to become a happy person rests in quality relationships. Whether it's business, personal or intimate, relationships are our life. Unless you are autistic, the majority of your time is spent thinking about relationships. It is our thinking default setting, in other words, what we most often think about, when we are not specifically thinking about anything. If you want to know how to become a happier person, you must know how to develop happier relationships.

However, how often do we stop to analyze our relationships? How do we know if our business, personal and especially intimate relationships are working? Here is a basic process that you can use to analyze and understand how to become a happy person in your relationships.

How to become a happy person in your relationships - Exercise

1. Objectively examine your relationship. Draw a line down a piece of paper and write out the benefits of being in this relationship versus the costs of being in this relationship.
2. Now imagine the other person's perspective and write out how you think they perceive you? Write out another benefits versus costs list about you from their perspective.
3. Examine both lists and weigh the individual benefits versus costs on both lists. Is it 50/50, 60/40, 70/30 etc. and in which direction. Now you have a more objective measure of how your relationship looks.
4. Write out the kind of relationship you are seeking. What will you and what will you not accept? Consider how to communicate this and analyze what are the characteristics of your own that you would need to improve on in order to forge a better relationship.

5. Write out an action plan specifically stating how you plan to make such changes and if possible, tell someone you can trust what you are going to do and ask them to keep you accountable to your goals. One way to do this would be to make a friendly but serious bet with the person who will keep you accountable.
6. Monitor yourself. Briefly write down each day the times when you acted in a way in which you are proud and in ways that you need to improve. Consider how you would improve on that action next time you are in a similar situation with that person.
7. Review your notes at the end of the week.

By committing to go through this process, you will be able to generate a much more objective view on how your relationship is operating. Focusing on what you can specifically do to improve your relationship will allow you to influence the dynamic and create much more positive interactions. After going through this process for at least one week, an additional step is to ask the other person if they have noticed any changes in the quality of your interactions in order to obtain feedback from their perspective. Then, if you like, incorporate that feedback into your action plan, and implement new strategies based on the additional feedback in the following week. Then review again at the end of the next week. You can decide how long you want to go through this process with that particular person.

If you feel the other person in the relationship is open to it, you may want to go through this process together.

If by going through the scaling process you feel that the relationship you are in is too toxic, and not worth salvaging, refer to the bonus companion article 'How to live a happier life - Abandoning toxic relationships'.

How to live a happier life - Abandoning toxic relationships

Aleks Psych: This will be hard to hear, but there are a few things I need to say.

Smart Alek: I know.

Aleks Psych: Look, it's not you it's me.

Smart Alek: I agree.

Aleks Psych: I just need some time on my own.

Smart Alek: I agree.

Aleks Psych: Then why did you insist I speak to you face to face.

Smart Alek: To watch you squirm.

Nothing brings greater happiness then successful relationships and nothing brings greater pain then unsuccessful relationships. This is why leaving a relationship in order to learn how to live a happier life is so difficult because most of us do not like hurting other people and by doing this we will feel uncomfortable emotions, such as guilt.

However, sometimes you must, you must hurt that person in order to free both of you and give yourself a new opportunity to learn how to live a happier life.

Positive Psychology Practitioners understand the importance of relationships. One of the saddest things I see through my work is when I am working with someone who is clearly miserable in regards to their relationship but does not have the courage to leave.

Now, if the client believes that both he or she and his or her partner is open to change, then it is still quite possible to create an amazing relationship and find happiness. However, when the client knows that their partner is not going to change and that they are simply not compatible due to different values and beliefs, what I guarantee you will find is a person who is at the very least, moderately unhappy.

How to live a happier life – Keys to help you decide why and how to leave a toxic relationship.

1. Be very honest when you write out the answer to these questions. Why am I still with (name)? What needs is he or she meeting? Do you feel secure when you are with them? Are you afraid of being alone? Are you assuming that you could never find anyone better? Do you feel unworthy of love? Are you fearful of the consequences? Is life easier with them in regards to finances or the family unit? Do you feel like you would be a failure? Are you afraid of what others would say? Are you afraid of the physical, mental or emotional safety of yourself or your children?

2. Write down what needs he or she is not meeting. What do I, and if applicable, my family deserve?

3. Write down everything you can think of that you have to plan for if you decide to leave. What would you need financially? Where could you stay? What social support resources could you find? Will you need the help of a lawyer, therapist, accountant or other professional? Does extended family need to become informed and if so, who? How do you minimize the involvement of people with whom you don't want to spend very much time?

4. (This step is especially important for those in a toxic relationship that could possibly have numerous negative consequences). Read about and speak to people who have been in your situation before and are now in a much happier place. Ask them how they handled any conflict, personal fears and consequences and what they specifically did to free themselves from their relationship. Ask them their answer to all the questions you have had to answer yourself. If you are in a relationship where there is a real

fear of physical, emotional, and mental harm, then I recommend you seek professional counseling from a specialist in the area of concern.

5. Either on your own, with a friend you trust, or a counselor if needed, create a step-by-step timeline of future issues that you will face and a solution to how you will handle each challenge you face.

6. If you are concerned that you will not be able to say the right thing at the right time, make sure you practice what you want to say several times before each major step. Practice out loud and as realistically as possible. Practice your responses to any difficult questions or scenarios that could occur, each time with full 100% commitment. Be aware that the actual scenario will not go exactly the way you plan it. The best mentality to have is to have three or four key things you want to say that you have rehearsed and then to politely leave as quickly as possible. Avoid arguing or trying to repeatedly justify your decision.

7. Tell everyone you trust what you are going to do and when. Decide on a particular time, be prepared to accept the fear you will feel and do it! You must be able to answer this question. Am I committed despite any possible consequences? Meeting in a public place is also advisable if you fear that the other person may become aggressive, abusive or manipulative.

8. Set specific future contact boundaries. If no children or financial obligations are involved, set very limited contact boundaries (no face to face, zero contact is preferred though a possible limited time phone call once or twice a week if you believe it is necessary). If children and financial matters are involved it may be more specific but limited (e.g. 2 phone calls a week, specific drop off times etc.) and stick to them for at least a month before possibly changing them.

If in any doubt in regards to these steps, I always recommend you seek professional assistance.

Communicating without judgment – It's a snap

Smart Alek: I am great at reading people. I can tell the difference between a loser and a winner in an instant.

Aleks Psych: How?

Smart Alek: Losers ask short questions.

Aleks Psych: (Sighing) What about winners?

Smart Alek: We make statements!

The one thing people are very good at doing is judging others. If we want to survive in the world, the conclusions we draw from other people's verbal and non-verbal behavior requires that we make quick decisions based on our snap judgments. A snap judgment is one we make about someone within the first several seconds of meeting that person.

What research has found is that the snap judgments we make about other people are usually very accurate in regards to whether we later end up developing positive relationships with that person or not. Be aware that our psychology in terms of how we perceive others is biased towards first impressions.

However, as powerful as first impressions are, it is important to realize that we all look at the world in our own unique way based on our own individual experiences and the beliefs we have created from those experiences. Therefore, the first impression you have of someone could be very different from the first impression they have of you. Then who is right and who is wrong? The answer is you are both right and you are both wrong.

This brings me to one of the biggest problems. The issue is that we all have our own way of looking at the world and the huge mistake that we unconsciously make most of the time is that we assume that other people see the world in the same way we do. Because we naturally assume that they follow the same rules, we believe that we can judge them based on those rules.

Every time you judge someone, remember that your psychology is biased. Whatever you say or think is a reflection of your belief system that you instinctively believe is right. However, if someone does something you disagree with, it does not necessarily make them wrong.

Rather than judging, if you want to understand someone, you should be asking why. Try to remain neutral and ask yourself 'why would they do that,' 'what is it specifically that I disagree with,' 'could I be looking at this the wrong way' and 'what would they say to me if I asked them why they did that.' If you really want to understand the person, I then suggest you politely and with a tone of curiosity ask them about their ideas and beliefs that form to create their psychology.

Ask them where did their beliefs come from and what kind of experiences did they have to shape those beliefs. What you will find is a whole other world of experiences and conclusions made from those experiences. In the process you just might be able to develop a deeper understanding of that person and develop an appreciation for them, despite any initial unfavorable snap judgments.

Communicating without judgment - Exercise: Over the next week, every time you find yourself automatically negatively judging someone, consider how your beliefs may be different from theirs and try to consider the situation from their perspective. If you get the chance to ask them about their ideas and beliefs, then do so. Then in a journal, write down the insights you build.

Language of emotion - Change the color of your world

Aleks Psych: Each emotion has its own kind of language.

Smart Alek: That is so true. When I feel love, I speak French, when I feel determined I speak German, and when I feel intelligent, I speak Latin.

The language of emotion creates the color of your world. A good metaphor to use is that of a filter, or lenses where lighter colors represent positive emotions and darker colors represent negative emotions. Each emotion also has a language of its own that comes through you when you are under its influence. The stronger the emotion, the stronger the language of emotion, and the more overall impact it has on the color of your lenses.

Have you noticed that when you are relaxed, you think and speak a certain way? The language of emotion is that of calmness, slowing down and appreciating things. When you are excited, the language of emotion compels you to speak passionately about possibilities, creative ideas and benefits. The language of emotion when you feel love will create an urge to speak lovingly.

Positive emotions have their own language, but then, so too do negative emotions. When someone is anxious, the language is of danger, pain and future catastrophes. When someone is angry, the language is of unfair obstacles and injustices. When someone is sad, the language is of loss and future hardships.

What is interesting as I am sure you have experienced, is that even when you know that you don't want to be thinking, feeling or acting that way, you may not be able to help it if the emotion is too intense. Have you ever felt so excited, you simply could not sit still? You might even be able to see that the person has lost interest in what you're saying but you can't help but keep talking. Have you ever felt so relaxed that nothing seemed to bother you, or so in love that you could not shut up!

Now positive emotions are great, but not always appropriate for the situation. Our negative emotions are designed to be reality checks and protect us from getting into situations that would create even further pain. However, our negative emotions sometimes go way beyond the appropriate reality check. We can be hijacked by them and speak that language of emotion too strongly and potentially ruin your own goals and relationships.

Have you ever been so anxious that you started creating all sorts of completely unrealistic and impossible catastrophic scenarios in your mind? Maybe a loved one was running late and you thought what if they were kidnapped. Or, have you ever gotten so angry in an argument that you started saying all sorts of hurtful, damaging and inappropriate things and you had no real evidence to support what you were saying but you had to win! Then they started doing the same thing and both of you got out of control. Or, do you remember suffering a saddening setback or a loss. Maybe that young love left you without ever giving you that kiss and you thought your life would always be garbage and you would be doomed to a life of bleak solitude.

Understanding the languages of the emotions you feel will allow you to navigate your own internal world with much more confidence and certainty. It will also allow you to accept, work through and learn from negative emotions more easily so you can swiftly return to positive experiences.

Language of Emotion - Exercise: Over the next week, whenever you feel the influence of a strong emotion, positive or negative, try to observe the language of emotion you are feeling. Notice the kind of ideas and thoughts that are running through your mind. Ask yourself: is this the appropriate emotion that I want to feel right now? If it is, then act on what you are thinking and enjoy. If it is not, ask yourself what emotion would I like to be in right now in order to handle this situation? If I was feeling that emotion (e.g. happy, confident, compassionate) what would I need to do? Then select the best idea and commit it to action.

Other Books and Resources and Review Options

Thank you for reading this speed happiness strategies book. My objective with this book is for your experience to feel like a coaching session where you spend minimal time reading and the majority of your time applying. If you liked what you read, I would appreciate your support. Please take a moment to leave a review of this book on Amazon. I value your feedback and it helps me to continue writing the kind of books that people want.

Help me to help you by helping me to help you with your review :) Go to: http://www.amazon.com/Aleks-Srbinoski/e/B005JWGWWY/

Would you like to develop other key areas of success in just 1-2 hours? Below is a list of where you can find more of my work.

To be informed of upcoming books, articles and podcasts visit **FulfillingHappiness.com** and join the mailing list.

Amazon Store: My author profile and available books are at: http://www.amazon.com/Aleks-Srbinoski/e/B005JWGWWY/

Other Kindle Ebooks (first also available in print) by Aleks:

Destiny Defining Decisions: 11 Best-Selling Entrepreneurs Reveal their Greatest Success Secrets (Entrepreneur Interview Series)

Motivation Now: Productivity and Persuasion Secrets For Modern Day Excellence and Effectiveness (60 Minute Success Series)

Instant Inner Calm: Simple Stress Management Strategies To Increase Clarity, Creativity and Calm (60 Minute Success Series)

Precision Language: Powerful and Precise Positive Thinking Secrets For Personal and Professional Success (60 Minute Success Series)

The 7 Mental Viruses Crushing Your Potential: Overcome Fear and Negative Thinking by Building a New Positive Mindset (60 Minute Success Series)

10 Life Success Secrets Revealed: Your Simple Guide To Success, Wealth and Fulfilling Happiness (60 Minute Success Series)

Coming Soon – First Release in January 2015

THE MENTAL HEALTH AND HAPPINESS SERIES
Free chapter on Goal Setting on following pages

Books will be available on Amazon or mass copies directly sought from the author.

Special Acknowledgements

Thank you again to the Elonera Montessori School staff and volunteers who helped run the challenge. You did an amazing job!

How to work with Aleks

Aleks George Srbinoski is an author, speaker and multidisciplinary psychologist focusing on mental health, success, happiness and entrepreneurship.

Known as a leading expert in success and happiness strategies, he is the founder of FulfillingHappiness.com and author of the Success Secrets Series, and the Fulfilling Happiness Program. Join his mailing list or use handle @AleksPsych to follow on twitter for regular updates.

He consults in person but also works with organizations and schools from all over the world through online training programs. Contact him via **aleks@fulfillinghappiness.com** to discuss how he may be able to assist you or your organization.

Goal Setting Bonus Chapter

As previously stated, the original inspiration behind *The Happiness Up, Stress Down Challenge* was a twist on New Year's Resolutions.

However, setting goals in the traditional sense is still important and very common, so I decided to add this chapter from my upcoming book to be released in the later part of January 2015.

It will be the first in a new series of books where I focus on how to maximize Mental Health and Happiness. In the first book, I outline 20 key principles for superior mental health and cover just about every core area required for optimal living and in overcoming depression, anxiety and related mental illness issues.

The book covers motivation, optimism, achievement, exercise, sleep, nutrition, relationships, social skills, mindfulness, peak performance, creating empowering beliefs and a confident self-image, positive thinking, meaningful living, how to boost mood and overcome anxiety and much more.

Enjoy your bonus chapter!

Aleks

Easy Goal Setting and Accountability

This is the simplest and easiest goal setting process you will ever come across so you can stop procrastinating and start succeeding

The clock continues to tick! Each reverberation of sound acts as a tiny dagger to the heart. She sits there paralyzed. There is so much inside, so much to offer, but where does she start? A few doors down he is feeling the exact same way, and so are countless others. They all hide behind distractions and excuses and the dream continues to slip away. One could have been a novelist, another a painter, one an engineer, and another a dancer. A week passes, a month, a year and even decades go by. Still the clock ticks, their hearts bleed and they remain still.

If only they just started, if they just made the first goals really small and built from there rather than fixating on the overall size of the aspiration. If only they took that step and told other supportive people of their authentic ambition rather than hiding in the shadows. If only … However, it is not too late! As long as a heart still beats, new creation is possible.

To be successful, you must set goals. When I say success, I am referring not just to your work, but to all aspects of your life. In the past, I have developed deep and detailed goal setting processes and it's possible to write an entire book on goal setting alone, but to dive into a highly detailed goal setting process now would be overwhelming and unnecessary.

This is a book of mental health developing principles. It is better to give you a process that is as streamlined as possible, so you can start now! One secret to success is to make your initial goals in any area as easy as possible so you can build momentum. Success breeds success.

My goal is for you to begin by setting 1-2 small and easy goals for yourself by the end of this section.

You can get on the right track now with a simple 3-step goal setting process. Before I reveal it, the question that needs to be answered is: Why is goal setting important? If you want to succeed at something, you must set a goal to do it. Think about it; just about everything you do in a day is achieved because you set a goal to do it. Brushing your teeth is a goal, eating lunch is a goal and getting to work on time is a goal.

The question is not do you set goals, the question is do you set empowering goals? How do you set empowering goals? By actually sitting down and asking yourself what is it that you really want in your life. It may help to break up your life into different categories so you have a more complete picture of your life.

You could break up your life into these basic categories.

Health

Finances

Career

Passions/Hobbies

Intimate Relationships

Family Relationships

Relationships Other

Then choose just one category to begin with. Let's take Passions/Hobbies.

Let's say you are an artist and your busy life is interfering with your ability to get your art project done. Here is how you could get your project done.

1. Estimate how long you actually think it would take to complete the project. If you are new to structured goal setting, then to be safe, add an extra 30-50% to the estimated time-frame.

Things almost always get in the way and it can be discouraging at first. If you are new to the process, considerably overestimate how long it will take. If you are wrong about your estimate and you get it done sooner, great, you can create a more accurate estimate for the next project.

2. Details, details, details. Be very specific about how and when you will do everything related to the goal. These are called sub-goals. The more specific you are, the more likely you are to follow through on the goal process each time.

For example, it could look something like this:

Tomorrow at 7am, I will get up and spend half an hour at the most examining my art supplies and taking inventory. In my lunch break at 12:30, I'll go to the art store and purchase everything I need for the project.

Tonight, immediately after dinner, I will clear my art study and prepare all materials. Then my regular procedure will be this.

Mon, Wed, Fri: Each session is a minimum of 1 hour up to a maximum of 2 hours. The aim will be about 1.5 hours. Each session will begin between 9 and 9:20pm and I must work on the project for at least one full hour regardless of how I am feeling.

I will set aside 10 minutes in the beginning for warm up creativity exercises and 10 minutes at the end for clean-up and preparation for the next session.

3. Review Progress – Each week until the goal is completed, spend the time needed to review progress and readjust the estimated time of completion.

For example, every Sunday night immediately after dinner, I will spend 10-20 minutes reviewing progress and setting expectations for the following week. As a highly recommended bonus, promise yourself a reward each week if you complete what you set out to do.

There you go, a very simple three-step goal setting process that you can begin immediately.

Goal Setting Exercise: Choose a goal and follow the process just outlined.

First, choose a category to focus on. Then follow the basic process explained.

1. Create a goal completion time-frame estimate.

2. Make your sub-goals as detailed and specific as possible and commit to them.

3. Review Progress by setting aside a particular time each week to do so.

I told you it was simple. However, setting a goal is not the same as committing to complete a goal. An intelligent goal setter will also set up accountability measures. To assist you here, I've outlined my 4 Ps of accountability.

4 Ps of A-level Accountability

Below are the 4 Ps of accountability and some quick strategies on how to best incorporate each of the principles. Be aware that they are in ascending level of power. In other words, the 4th P is the highest level of accountability, but all four are beneficial and work best when all utilized together.

The 4 Ps are:
- **Personal accountability**
- **Partner accountability**
- **Party accountability**
- **Public accountability**

The first person you have to be accountable to is "you." As part of this stage you are to get clear on your compelling reasons for pursuing the goal and write out a list of the benefits of obtaining the goal and consequences of not obtaining it. Then narrow the list to the top five most emotionally intense benefits and consequences.

Place the list in a highly visible place or in multiple places and review frequently.

To enhance personal accountability, consider crafting a mission statement, creating a scrapbook with relevant images, journaling on your commitment, and developing a set of beliefs, rules, and expectations that you verbally declare to follow through on a regular basis. Put as many positive reminders of the goal in your environment as possible.

The next level up is becoming accountable to a "partner." Being vulnerable and declaring your goals in front of another person is difficult.

What you want at this level is someone who is supportive, trustworthy, positive, but also firm. Your partner **CAN NOT** be an "it's okay" kind of person. You have to hate the idea of disappointing them, as they will not be accepting of any run-of-the-mill excuses.

Checking in on a regular basis, preferably daily, is best and to enhance the process, making friendly bets should be incorporated. The bet should offer a nice reward if you succeed and a reasonably annoying and irritating consequence if you do not. For example, if you are successful, your partner takes you out to your favourite restaurant, but if you fail you have to wash their car every week for a month.

The next level is to be accountable to a "party." Having not just one person but a group of people you are committed to will add support and usually increase compliance. Especially if you are in the right kind of group who all share similar beliefs, attitudes and are determined to succeed. Everything you do with a partner you can also do with a group, but now you are committed to more people.

The highest level of accountability is "public." This is where you do everything you can to tell everyone about your goal. Everyone you meet should know about it. It should be revealed across websites and social media channels, and questions from whomever must be encouraged and welcomed. You should brand yourself with your goal, perhaps making T-shirts and other paraphernalia related to it. At this level, it may even become a cause.

You may notice that this is what many celebrities will do if they have really struggled with a certain goal, usually weight loss. They will declare it publicly through the media and advertising. With so many people now aware of the goal, the potential pain and embarrassment for not succeeding is very high, but also the potential support and pleasure for succeeding is magnified many times over. Another example of accountability at this level is entering competitions or starting goal-related groups. When you go public, you have the opportunity to be a role-model and make a real positive social impact.

Success at this level is guaranteed to increase self-esteem, confidence, and pride. Even if only a few people learn of and actively support your efforts, your frequent public declarations show just how serious and committed you are. Those are the 4 Ps. Ideally, you want to cater to all four levels. Consider a goal you currently have and work through this process.

Principle Summary

Easy Goal Setting and accountability: This is the simplest and easiest goal setting process you will ever come across so you can stop procrastinating and start succeeding.

The more specific and detailed you make your goal, the easier it is follow. Writing it down and setting up accountability measures will dramatically increase chances of success.

Fast-Action Techniques

1. Write down three goals you would like to achieve over the next year. Then narrow it down to just one, whichever is most authentically important to you at this time of your life. Write it down three times (attach related images as well if you like) and place each piece of paper in three different and highly visible places. Then write a long list of benefits of achieving the goal and consequences of not obtaining it.

2. Do the three-step goal set process. Estimate total length of time required for completion, write out a detailed plan of actions and a scheduled weekly review time to adjust sub-goals and finish date as you progress. Finally, reward yourself at the end of each weekly review.

3. Set up your accountability measures and partners. You can start simply with only a few measures (as long as it will keep you committed), but aim to continually build your accountability measures over time. Only start an additional major goal after you have set up what you need and are confident of maintaining the first. Then repeat all above steps again for the next goal and so on.

Did you enjoy this chapter? The complete book with all 20 principles will be released at the end of January 2015.

Amazon Store: My author profile and available books are at: **http://www.amazon.com/Aleks-Srbinoski/e/B005JWGWWY/**

9362924R00083

Printed in Great Britain
by Amazon.co.uk, Ltd.,
Marston Gate.